On Reading
Karl Barth
in
South Africa

Edited by

Charles Villa-Vicencio

GRAND RAPIDS, MICHIGAN
WILLIAM B. EERDMANS PUBLISHING COMPANY

Library of Congress Cataloging-in-Publication Data

On reading Karl Barth in South Africa / edited by Charles Villa-Vicencio.
    p.   cm.
   ISBN 0-8028-0320-2
   1. Barth, Karl, 1886–1968.
   2. Church and state—South Africa—History—20th century.
   3. Theology, Doctrinal—South Africa—History—20th century.
   I. Villa-Vicencio, Charles.
   BX4827.B3052   1988
   261.7′0968—dc19   88-7153
                                    CIP

Contents

Preface

Academic theology has tended to emerge from the dominant groups of society and be entrenched on the side of the status quo in various situations throughout the world. In South Africa and elsewhere it has long been used to legitimate the existing order. This tendency has not, however, been able to suppress a residual protest against this kind of monopolization of theology by the existing order. The gospel, as the good news to the poor and the liberation of the oppressed, is the essence of this protest—and any exercise in reclaiming theology for the poor and oppressed involves the celebration of this protest.

The work of some theologians within the dominant theological tradition provides a liberating resource to overcome the appropriation of theology for the benefit of the powerful. But this resource is often obscured by such theologians' excessive concern with matters of dogma, as dictated by the milieu from which they emerge. The reclaiming of a theological heritage involves identifying the contradictory dimensions of a particular theology and developing the liberating resources within that tradition.

This volume constitutes an exercise by theologians fundamentally opposed to the existing political order in South Africa, who categorically reject any theological attempt to come to terms with it, to reclaim the theology of Karl Barth. We hope there will be similar efforts to reread other traditional theological resources, addressing to them a number of questions that have arisen from an encounter with liberation theologians writing out of situations of oppression worldwide.

Dirkie Smit's essay provides the framework within which the other essays are located—namely, the paradigm of God's radical grace in Jesus Christ. My essay on the revolution of God considers the implications of this for sociopolitical revolution. Robin Petersen further develops this theme in his discussion of Barth's lifelong commitment to economic socialism, and Alan Brews deals with Barth's attitude toward violence within the context of political change. Chuck Wanamaker considers the biblical basis of Barth's understanding of church-state relations. Each of these essays offer certain explicit insights into church-state relations in the South African context.

Nico Horn compares the Barmen Declaration, which formed the basis of the Confessing Church's resistance to Hitler's Nazi regime, with the Nederduitse Gereformeerde Sendingkerk's Belhar Confession and the Kairos Document in the South African context. Jaap Durand's essay contrasting the views of Karl Barth and Abraham Kuyper provides a historical study on the theological milieu within Afrikaner theology, and John de Gruchy's contribution on the church struggle provides a critical assessment of Barth's theology in relation to contemporary church-state issues.

Mary Armour has assisted me greatly in editing these manuscripts, and Pat Lawrence has generously furnished the necessary secretarial skills. I am greatly indebted to them both. I am especially grateful to Allan Boesak, a good friend who has never tired of affirming the theological basis of the oppressed people's quest for human dignity and political liberation. His Foreword locates this volume in a context of struggle, beyond the pages of academic writing, in which theory and praxis find unity.

I suggest in the introductory essay that Barth's theology has reached the church in this country through the filter of Protestant orthodoxy. Many who have discovered the "other" Barth, the Barth of this volume, have been nurtured in this process by the writings of Paul Lehmann. His writings on Barth have exerted explicit influence on much that is contained between the covers of this book, and his important volume *The Transfiguration of Politics* has had formative influence on several of the contributors to this anthology. Professor Lehmann has never visited this country, and none of us have had the pleasure of studying under him. His work, however, constitutes an essential ingredient in the reclaiming of the theological heritage within which we stand. On the hundredth anniversary of Karl Barth's birth, Paul Lehmann celebrated his eightieth birthday. We take great pleasure in dedicating this collection of South African essays to him.

CAPE TOWN   CHARLES VILLA-VICENCIO
SEPTEMBER 1986

Foreword

The Christian heritage is riddled with contradictions. It speaks of a God of love and justice, although it has been appropriated by successive generations of oppressors to exploit the black majority of this land. When whites first seized the land on this southern tip of Africa and initiated a process of the systematic oppression of its indigenous people, they did so in the name of the Christian God. Today, more than three hundred years later, the South African government, guilty beyond any doubt before the bar of history, condemned by every major political forum in the world, and judged guilty of sin and heresy by every major Christian church in the world, still dares to call itself Christian. The name of God is enshrined in the constitution of this white republic, the ruling party sanctifies its meetings with prayer, and whites who support this government in droves manage to rank among the highest church-going populations of the world. This is South Africa—both oppressive and religious.

Missionaries successfully implanted Christianity among the black population of this country. The debate about the sociopolitical consequences of this process is a long and controversial one. Whatever the intentions of those who came bearing the "good news," and despite the immediate concerns shown at the level of philanthropic care, the message that was preached in the name of Christ was one of submission and passivity. "The rich man in his castle, the poor man at the gate, God made them high and lowly, and ordered their estate" are the words of a hymn sung in mission stations across South Africa. The promised reward awaiting the patient and meek recipients of this faith was a crown in heaven. What is saddest of all is that there are still oppressed people in this country who believe this message, accept their inferior status in life, and internalize their oppression in the guise of a form of Christian piety.

The gospel of Christ is, however, more powerful than the wiles of those who conveniently appropriate it to their own ends. The history of black prophets, the emergence of the independent church, and the protest of black historic and black mission churches in this country witness to a gospel that is *good news for the poor and the oppressed* and that has been heard, albeit by a minority of people, from the very beginning. Indeed some who heard the gospel understood it better than those who preached it. In more recent times the emergence of black and liberation theology in South Africa bears further witness to a gospel of liberation hidden within the distortions of white imperialist religion. The story is too long to be told here, but individuals—both black and white—and groups of people from different Christian traditions have heard this gospel throughout the history of this country. The high-water marks of this tradition are few but precious: the Cottesloe Conference, the emergence of the Christian Institute, *The Message to the People of South Africa,* the founding of ABRECSA, the Belydendekring, the Apartheid Is a Heresy Declaration, the June 16 Theological Rationale, and the Kairos Document. The support for these events and statements among oppressed people in this country affirms a different gospel from the one preached in so many of the major pulpits of this land.

The pertinent question is, "Which is the gospel of the poor man of Galilee?" There are two gospels preached not only in this country, but in numerous countries around the world. There is a gospel for the rich and powerful and a gospel for the poor and lowly. The strength of black liberation theology both in South Africa and in North America is its systematic rejection of "traditional" and "white" theology, by which is meant that theology which favors the existing order of oppression. What some have called a "new way of doing theology" is in fact not new at all. We have rather identified, revitalized, and reappropriated the gospel we read about in the Bible, which our oppressors have distorted and idolatrously used to legitimate their own selfish ends.

This volume, designed to repossess the Christian heritage *for* the oppressed and, as Barth has said so definitely, "against the exalted . . . [and] against those who have rights," is a vitally important step in the reappropriation exercise. It constitutes a bold new step in the contemporary theological debate. The contributors to this volume use the insights and lessons of black and liberation theology to reread traditional theology, in this instance Karl Barth's theology. And the outcome? In essence, an unqualified affirmation of what the poor have instinctively always known and what contextual theologians witness to: that God is the God of the poor. This means that for theology to be true to the gospel it has to favor the interests of the poor. When one reads the essays in this book, one realizes that Charles Villa-Vicencio is correct when he writes that it is "not only the future [that] belongs to those in quest of sociopolitical liberation, but also significant, neglected, or misinterpreted parts of our theological heritage." This is good news to the poor. It also witnesses to the gross misuse of the Christian tradition by Christian spokespersons for the oppressors of this world, not least among whom are Christian ministers, theological teachers, and other servants of the church.

I am grateful to the authors of the essays that appear in this book. Their contribution can only make for a more fruitful dialogue between liberation and traditional theologies. This is a courageous publication. Reappropriation, whether of material, cultural, or theological resources, is never an easy task, and it dare never be triumphalistic. It is, however, vitally important. It seeks to restore to its rightful owners what has been taken from them. The gospel was first preached to the poor, and to them it must be restored. We are now discovering that many of the theological resources that consistently have been used in this country against us are in fact important resources in our struggle for spiritual and political liberation. This systematic exercise in reclaiming Barth could be the first step in a new theological era in South Africa.

I have often recognized in Barth's writings a strangely contemporary ring, and have used them in my own theology. These essays ought to be read by every serious student of theology around the world. There is something very important happening in this volume. Charles Villa-Vicencio has served us well in initiating this study.

I am grateful for the opportunity to be associated with this project and am particularly happy to celebrate not only the hundredth birthday of Karl Barth but the eightieth birthday of Paul Lehmann. Professor Lehmann's theology has had a profound influence on my theological pilgrimage, and I rate his *Transfiguration of Politics* among the most formative theological studies I ever read. That a collection of South African essays, dedicated to this remarkable man, should focus on Barth within a South African context and be written by theologians who are dissidents in respect to both the prevailing political order and the dominant oppressive theology in South Africa, represents an appropriate statement about him. Professor Lehmann is a superb scholar, he has an enduring interest in South Africa, and all that he believes and is, is at variance with the established world order of political and economic dominance. I share with the other contributors to this volume in saluting one of the truly great theologians and people of this century, a remarkable teacher and a good friend.

CAPE TOWN   ALLAN BOESAK
SEPTEMBER 1986

Introduction: Reclaiming the Christian Heritage

Charles Villa-Vicencio

South Africa is an intensely religious country. Ever since the arrival of the first white settlers and missionaries, Christianity has been used to legitimate white rule. This appropriation of the Christian tradition to justify an emerging or existing order is not peculiar to South Africa; religion is used in many parts of the world to fire the imperium of nations. Nor is it a phenomenon unique to any one era of South African history. The early Dutch settlers spoke of bringing their gift of civilization and the gospel to the heathen. The British occupation of the Cape was similarly interpreted as a God-given responsibility to introduce the values of Western Christian civilization to the indigenous peoples. Yet no regime in South Africa has legitimized its policy of the subjection of the black majority as explicitly and with the same theological resolve as have the Afrikaner nationalists since coming to power in 1948. The English-speaking churches must, however, shoulder some of the responsibility along with the Afrikaner regime. While they have not indulged in the same kind of theologizing of apartheid as their Afrikaner counterparts, the English-speaking churches have in practice allowed racial segregation to intensify in both church and state while they have pursued a sterile theology that has failed to address the political rigors of the day. These churches are as guilty of the heresy of the praxis of apartheid as the Afrikaans churches have ever been of the heresy of the doctrine of apartheid.[1]

One cannot fully understand this historical process of subjugation without comprehending the extent to which the Christian tradition has been appropriated and used to legitimate white domination and exploitation. This appropriation has caused some people in this

1

country deliberately to turn away from Christianity, rejecting it as "the religion of whites," while the Bible and the rifle have come to be seen as joint symbols of subjugation. Others have clung to the faith imparted to them by the missionaries, often questioning the authenticity of the faith of their oppressors but accepting their "place" in society while striving for an escape from this life by means of an ethereal brand of religion.

An alternative and contradictory understanding of faith has, however, existed alongside this dominant form of Christianity from the beginning of the colonial period. This countertradition has resulted in several individuals and groups rising up in protest against the existing order in the church. It has given rise to the African Indigenous Churches, movements such as the now banned Christian Institute, various declarations of faith such as the Cottesloe Statement (1961), the *Message to the People of South Africa* (1968), and the Ottawa heresy declaration by the World Alliance of Reformed Churches (1982).[2] Other black, liberation, and African theologies have similarly given expression to this tradition of protest against both explicit forms of apartheid theology and less obvious forms of traditional theological acquiescence to the existing order. And most recently, this alternative faith has found expression in the Kairos Document.

The purpose of this book is to share in the process of identifying this alternative faith as it appears in some of the major resources of the Christian tradition. Recognizing that this alternative or liberating faith has been suppressed by generations of imperialist theology, it must be redefined and reappropriated by that church which stands in solidarity with the poor.

On Reclaiming a Theological Tradition

The debate concerning the appropriation and repossession of symbols is an enduring one. Is it ever possible to turn religious symbols and theological resources the right-way up and use them against their appropriators? Or, as some have suggested, is theology always a resource serving the dominant class and oppressive by nature?[3] Can theology be used against those who have for so long used it to appease and oppress the masses? The answer is partly to be found in the emergence of a "theology of the poor" that has found a foothold in institutional churches around the world—although this kind of theology has always existed within the church of the poor. Theology *is* being used against its appropriators. In South Africa this exercise is proving itself to be an inherent part of the political revolution of our times. As a result of this the state is persecuting, with an intensity not hitherto felt in this country, that part of the church which seeks to stand in solidarity with the poor.

This radical confrontation between different theological perceptions, linked as it is to different class structures while cutting across denominational barriers, has forced many theologians to realize that the pursuit of knowledge can never be a disinterested end in itself. As a result some theologians, once content to isolate themselves from the influence of the social sciences, are turning to these sciences in an effort to explain their own differences in perception.[4] Three momentous consequences have followed from this shift.

First, theologians have been forced to realize that theology always serves the interests of some individual, some group, or some particular end that an individual or group has in mind: the interests of the state, the wealthy, the poor, academic prestige, or a particular political ideal.

Second, they have been forced to realize that it is impossible to maintain a neutral position in the pursuit of knowledge. Society is always moving culturally, economically, and sociopolitically in a certain direction. To try to remain neutral is to allow this movement to continue unchecked and uncorrected. It is to support the status quo by default.

Third, what a theologian discovers in a text is largely determined by the position he or she occupies in society. What has revolutionized theology in recent times is the fact that the theological reflection of oppressed people has penetrated the theological marketplace, and this kind of theology is very different from that expressed by theologians who have emerged from the dominant class. The world of traditional theology is still endeavoring to come to grips with this reality.

The theology of the poor begins with an existential awareness of society very different from the experience of the wealthy. And when the Bible is read from this location, it yields certain insights that have been denied the most erudite, meticulous, and learned scholars through centuries of church history. A theologian needs to be poor to appreciate fully the words, nuances, and images of the Bible pertaining to hunger, denial of shelter, and a lack of material security. A theologian needs to experience the reality of prison to discover the number of times "prison" is actually referred to in the Acts of the Apostles. A theologian needs to be oppressed to discover how dominant is the theme of liberation in the Bible.

The explanation for this process of discovery is simple enough. It has to do with reading a text from a different perspective. What we find in the Bible is determined by our most urgent needs. To favor the perspective of the poor in contemporary debate does not constitute a denial of the pursuit of "objective" truth; it is rather an exercise *in* the pursuit of truth. It constitutes an attempt to include that dimension of truth which had hitherto been excluded from the pursuit of truth.[5] More than this, the interests of the poor are a corrective to the interests of the dominant classes, insofar as the latter are the interests of domination and exploitation which are not necessarily in the interests of society as a whole. When theologians affirm a "preferential option" for the poor, they are affirming an option against domination.

This commitment to the poor and the radically different kind of theology that results from it are further attributable to the recognition that the formative experiences underlying the Bible and the history of the church were based on situations of persecution and oppression common to the poor everywhere and at all times. In other words, one needs to be part of the crisis of oppression and to live on the edge of existence to perceive and understand the resources of the Christian tradition which bear witness to such events.

Theologians who are not poor and not of the oppressed community have, through heightened awareness and theological relocation, learned these insights from the poor and the oppressed. In seeking to show solidarity with this community of people by joining them in their struggle, they have occasionally come to experience some measure of the oppression the poor experience by birth. These theologians have also come to recognize that the biblical tradition *requires* those who seek to be obedient to the prophetic tradition and who desire to be followers of Jesus to be in solidarity with the poor and oppressed, using their skills to serve the interests of the oppressed. Míguez-Bonino speaks of the "double-location" of the Christian theologian. The theologian, he argues, occupies a particular socio-economic place in society, but also a theological location that obliges him or her to be in the service of the poor.[6] This requires the theologian who is true to this particular tradition within the church to work in close proximity with the oppressed people of society, to hear *their* questions, to respond to *their* needs, and, as far as possible, to fear *their* fears and dream *their* dreams that emerge from *their* oppression and *their* poverty.

The authors of the essays in this book wrote with this aim in mind. We have reapproached a particular figure in our theological heritage, in this case Karl Barth, with a set of questions in mind that are vastly different from those we inherited from our teachers. These concerns, to the extent that we are able to understand them, articulate some of the questions, needs, fears, and hopes of the oppressed people of this country. Our intention is to uncover a hidden tradition of the church and to reclaim some of those resources that traditional theologians in this country have allowed to slip by unnoticed—or have simply regarded as unimportant. We have discovered that what has until now been regarded as secondary in the theology of Barth—namely, his quest for a theological basis for his sociopolitical engagement—is, in fact, primary. We are also discovering that this is true not only with regard to the theology of Karl Barth but also with regard to the theology of many of the great theologians. Indeed, not only the future belongs to those in quest of sociopolitical liberation, but also significant, neglected, or misinterpreted parts of our theological heritage from the past.

A New Theological Phase

Contextual theology is necessarily grounded in the history and culture of the situation out of which it emerges: slavery, racial discrimination, and capitalism have shaped the identity of North American black theology, while economic exploitation, colonization, and the history of Roman Catholic mission work have helped mold the identity of Latin American liberation theology. Black, African, and liberation theologies in South Africa have all, to varying degrees, been influenced by African precapitalist culture, while their *raison d'être* has been their opposition to both apartheid and the experience of faith as mediated by the history of missions. Missionary theology and later theological influences within the Protestant tradition—suitably digested by seminary and university teachers—continue to shape the theological identity of the majority of both black and white parish ministers in the mainline Protestant churches in this country.

This situation explains the importance of reclaiming this tradition for the benefit of liberation. This tradition exercises a profound influence in the church, and it cannot be left unredeemed as traditional theologians have imparted it to us. Nor, in the interests of the truthful transmission of the history of the Christian tradition, can we allow certain important theological insights into the political quest for freedom and basic social justice to be lost.

A new phase of theology is emerging in South Africa. It has to do with a rapprochement between liberation theology and traditional theologies. Most theological exercises move through three clearly demarcated phases, and the liberation theology debate in South Africa has been no exception. The rebirth of theology so closely associated

5

with the liberation theology debate both here and abroad began with a deliberate rejection of traditional theological resources in order to affirm what was hailed as an epistemological break with the past. This constituted a prophetic celebration of an entirely "new way" of doing theology. It was followed by a period of systematization and internal critique in which the identity of this "new way" of doing theology was established as a methodology in its own right, a basic alternative to the existing form of traditional theology. A further phase has now emerged. As internally directed critical questions raised by liberation theologians have stubbornly defied satisfactory answers in the sociopolitical and economic revolutions of our times, traditional theologies, which have addressed their own crises and stood the test of time, are being reread with these specific questions in mind. This new set of questions has produced a new set of responses from traditional theology, making possible a dialogue between these two kinds of theology that is creatively different from the earlier stance of mutual exclusion. This process is perhaps nowhere more clearly evident than in the June 16 Theological Rationale calling on Christians to pray for the removal of unjust rulers in South Africa, first published in 1985. It is, however, also seen in the debate that has raged in relation to the Kairos Document, as individuals and groups have not only attacked it using traditional theological resources but also defended it with the help of the same resources![7]

Justifiable and necessary as the rejection of traditional theological resources might have been in the early development of African, black, and liberation theologies in this country, these new insights also need to be considered in relation to traditional theologies. Differently stated, even though there have been valid reasons for rejecting traditional resources, there remain equally valid reasons for repossessing them. In so doing, the danger always exists that the decisive new ground gained will simply be absorbed into the existing order, while the decisive prophetic insights are compromised. Alternatively, if the new insights are indeed valuable, they will help to identify and renew what is good in all that is past. In the process it will be shown that many of the traditional theological resources are *also* supportive of the liberation of the oppressed. There is then but one step needed to confirm what the oppressed have always known: that the oppressors of this world have never had the Christian tradition on their side, but have deceitfully used it to baptize their own selfish and ungodly ends.

The Abuse of Traditional Theology

What has become clear in recent times is that leading theologians have often been incorrectly used (and often abused), directly or by implication, to legitimate oppression in this country. Clearly many imperialist theologians in the Christian tradition have written their theology from the perspective of the ruling class and for the benefit of the rulers. Some theologians have consistently or at particular moments explicitly legitimated the exploitation and even the massacre of the poor. Other traditional theologians, however, have consciously sought to represent the needs and aspirations of the poor, although they frequently have failed to translate their noblest theological and ethical ideals into praxis. In so doing they failed to cross that epistemological gap that separates them from liberation theology. But this does not mean that they were not provided with theological resources that can be appropriated by those whose theology *is* grounded in praxis. Still other theologies carry within them potentially liberative forces overshadowed by other interests or not yet fully developed. Today these ideals and often obscured forces are being discerned within the larger theological tradition and reappropriated by those who believe that the gospel is ultimately a gospel for the poor and the oppressed. So, to cite but a single example, while Augustine's theology has often been used in the West to legitimate the existing political order, a more radical reading has emerged in which certain ideas within Augustine's theology are taken away from the theologians of the status quo and used for the liberation of the oppressed.[8]

In South Africa no theologian has been more consistently appropriated by the forces of oppression than John Calvin—and this in direct contradiction to the major thrust of his thought. Other theologians, in turn, have been indirectly used to legitimate the existing order by default. A postgraduate black student recently discovered the liberating resources in Karl Barth's theology for the first time. "I've been lied to for all these years," he said. "My seminary teachers never told me Barth was a socialist!" Even the most well-meaning and able disciples of great thinkers fall short in representing the full range and potential of their mentor's theological resources and only too often end by focusing on certain aspects of the literature in an ahistorical manner, thus distorting what they claim to interpret.

Many of the theological resources used in church and educational institutions have been selected and taught in such a way that traditional concerns outweigh liberating dimensions. When these liberating aspects are ignored by teachers and preachers who have no real need or ability to emphasize them, oppressed people are justified in turning away from these resources. To do justice to a text, however, the reader should enquire about the context out of which it emerged. When Barth's writings are read with this requirement in mind certain liberating resources immediately become apparent. Of course theologians of former times and differing contexts cannot be expected to provide answers to the specific questions that confront the church in South Africa today. But people who are aware of the context in which their theology is grounded and who address their own set of questions of ultimacy in an authentic manner also address universal questions of ultimacy. In so doing they help us respond in an authentic manner to our own contextual questions about the ultimate purpose of our existence. When these people have been compelled by accidents of history to face crises similar to ours, and happen to be predecessors of the tradition within which we stand, then the importance of their journey through life takes on added significance for our own. We read and explore the thought and existential identity of others in order that we may learn from them how to deal with the challenges that face us. Certain important events, significant symbols, and charismatic figures become "windows" into our own identity and possibly even into ultimate reality itself. Figures like Karl Barth function for us in precisely this way—especially in the case of Barth, since he is part of our own theological development in South Africa.

Certainly in South Africa "Barthian" theology has, generally speaking, failed to grasp the pathos of Barth's own existential involvement in the crises of history through which he lived. Barth's theology has been taught, as so much theology has been taught in this country, within the confines of "Protestant orthodoxy." This theological process reaches back to the period of seventeenth-century Protestant scholasticism when a continuum of confessions of faith emerged in Reformed theological circles. These include the formulations of the Synod of Dort (1619) and the Westminster Confession (1647), influential in conservative Reformed circles in South Africa. Earlier Reformed confessions such as the Belgic Confession (1560), the Scots Confession (1560) written largely by John Knox, and the Heidelberg Catechism (1563), however, provide a more dynamic understanding of the Protestant tradition—and it was on these formulations that Barth wrote most extensively. His Gifford Lectures (1937 and 1938) were, for example, on the Scots Confession, and in 1948 he published a doctrinal commentary on the Heidelberg Catechism.[9]

Confessions of faith were orginally intended to serve as "guides and often as dikes against distortion."[10] Then came the threat of internal division within the emergent Protestant church, along with the process of sectarianism and the renewed vigor of Roman Catholicism that followed after the Council of Trent (1563) and the work of religious orders such as the Jesuits (founded in 1540).[11] In response to these forces, Protestantism began to take refuge in a brand of "scholasticism" that was in some ways not very different from the brand of medieval dogma against which it had earlier rebelled. It demanded assent to truth in certain deductive propositional forms that could be applied to different and changing situations. Protestantism had changed drastically. The dynamic theological quest of Luther and Calvin was arrested by a preoccupation with whether or not a particular formulation was true to a particular Confession of Faith. And in the process this concern for what was truly Protestant quite ironically led to "statements which differed from the *spirit* of Luther and Calvin."[12] The importance of contextual urgency was lost, and the theological vibrancy of the first generation reformers gave way to the passivity of later generations of Protestants who lived off the inheritance of their forebears. This religious milieu set the stage for the white settlement of the Cape, which began in 1652.

The story of the transmission of Protestantism from Europe to South Africa is told elsewhere.[13] It is enough to note that this kind of Reformed orthodoxy shaped the faith of many of the early Dutch settlers in the Cape. After the British occupation of the Cape, the British authorities were not inclined to allow Dutch ministers to enter the colony and arranged instead for Scottish Presbyterian ministers to meet the shortage of ministers in the Dutch Reformed Church. Today the name of Andrew Murray is a revered name in Dutch Reformed Church circles, and the pietism of the Reformed tradition continues to exercise a significant influence therein. It has been convincingly argued that what dissent has emerged within Afrikaner church circles over the years needs to be traced to this piety.[14] Yet, in the end, piety focuses on the personal and often private experience of faith. This, perhaps more than any other factor, left the way open for the deductive religion of Protestant orthodoxy to occupy the public space of politics and culture. One consequence was the emergence of a synthesis between theology and Afrikaner nationalism.

This public Reformed orthodoxy would in time be further developed in relation to a particular interpretation put on the Dutch Calvinism of the nineteenth-century theologian and Netherlands prime minister, Abraham Kuyper. Kuyper argued that there exists an autonomy or sovereignty that resides within the separate spheres of life—areas such as family, business, science, art, and so forth. His original concern was to limit the interference of government within these areas of life, arguing that an "innate law of life" and a "common grace" operates within these spheres as a "divine mandate."[15] In so doing Kuyper affirmed what had become a fairly standard Reformed concern to have as little government as possible. This would in time be developed further by Kuyper and later by the Dutch philosopher Herman Dooyeweerd into a "life-system" governing the interrelationship between the different spheres of existence.

But in the South African context this Kuyperian-Dooyeweerdian system was soon further developed to legitimate separate cultures, ethnic identities, languages, living areas—and the entire apartheid philosophy of life. *Soevereiniteit in eie kring* (autonomy within each sphere) and the celebration of *die eie* (one's own) became the theological and political battle cries of the Afrikaner's rise to power and later the cornerstones of "separate development." Each nation and each people, separate and distinct from each other, came to be regarded as a preordained, sacred entity to be protected and safeguarded at all costs as one's Christian responsibility. Of course this theology had significant similarities with German Christian *Ordnungstheologie*. Yet, because Kuyper's cosmology was so closely bound up with orthodox Reformed Christology, it was more difficult to discern the natural theology within this brand of Reformed thought than it had been for Barth and Bonhoeffer to identify such trends within the dominant theology of Nazi Germany. Jaap Durand speaks for many dissident theologians in South Africa when he writes: "One of the great tragedies in the development of Afrikaner Reformed theology in the three decisive decades of its development (1930–1960) was that Karl Barth's criticism of religion and of natural theology was never really heard or given any opportunity to be heard in those Kuyperian circles that needed it most."[16]

Theological development in the English-speaking churches of South Africa remained firmly rooted abroad, in Britain and North America, throughout this period. It did not become entrapped in questions of theologized nationalism, but neither was it nearly as interesting. With few exceptions, English-speaking theologians remained engrossed in questions of doctrinal niceties; their occasional deviations into matters of immediate concern carried with them a *laissez-faire* attitude. English-speaking theologians could afford to find their theological identity elsewhere, and not a single piece of significant theological writing emerged from these churches prior to the 1960s.

It was only as these churches in South Africa were forced by the events of Sharpeville, the rise of black consciousness, and the intensification of the black struggle for liberation to address political issues with some sense of urgency that theology began to emerge as a prophetic resource used to contradict the oppressive status quo. The late sixties saw the first writings on black theology emerge in South Africa.[17] Much of this work dismissed the Reformed and other traditions in the church, and many contextual theologians continue to do so. Others continued to draw on traditional sources within their contextual theologies from the beginning. Certainly the dominant roles played in the church in South Africa by Beyers Naudé, as a self-consciously Reformed theologian, and Desmond Tutu, who is in many ways a "traditional" Anglican, have always kept the traditional theological resources at the center of the political involvement of the church. Yet it is perhaps Allan Boesak who has done most to reclaim the Reformed tradition as part of the black struggle for liberation. In recent times it has been ABRECSA (Alliance of Black Reformed Christians in South Africa), the Belydendekring, the Belhar Confession of the N. G. Sendingkerk, and the publication of Allan Boesak's *Black and Reformed* which witness to a Reformed faith in South Africa on the side of the oppressed.[18]

This book, written during the centenary year of Karl Barth's birth, stands within this tradition as a protest against the manner in which Barth has been taught and used in this country without due concern for the central place he occupied in the resistance of the Confessing Church against Hitler in the 1930s.

Beginning with Karl Barth

Barth, we will argue, has not been sufficiently influential in the South African context. So why choose him in reclaiming a theological tradition? There are four contextual reasons. First, there is increasing evidence of a rediscovery of Barth by liberation theologians, recognizing what Míguez-Bonino has identified as the "dangerous tendency" in liberation theology to collapse the love of God into the love of neighbor with the effect of "deifying history or humanity itself." Barth's uncompromising affirmation and critique of the qualitative difference between God and humanity, and his critique of human revolutions from the perspective of God's revolution, needs to be taken into consideration by all liberation theologians.[19] Second, a sociotheological analysis shows that Barth's own theological pilgrimage, in which he sought an adequate theological basis for his own social action, contains disturbing theological insights for the church in South Africa today.[20] Third, for all the inadequacies of the manner in which Barth has been taught in this country, there are few, if any, theologically trained parish ministers of any denomination who are not familiar with certain categories of Barth's theology. Barth therefore provides a viable starting point for reclaiming a tradition. Even ministers who are indifferent to theological issues remain curious as to what it is that has made the "dogmatic" Barth of their fleeting seminary acquaintance the most acclaimed theologian of this century! Fourth, 1986 was the centenary year of Barth's birth. Some theologians saw this as sufficient reason to dust off their Barth volumes and reread at least some of his many words through a pair of lenses optically shaped and ground by the advent of a theology of the poor and oppressed. This exercise has led people to rediscover that Karl Barth is closer to us than are many Barthians indifferent to the struggle for social justice. We have caught a glimpse as to why Barth objected to being called a Barthian!

Barth was on one occasion out walking in Basel. On passing a bookstore that displayed his books, he apparently observed to his graduate assistant, "I hope nobody reads all this. At most it ought to provide merely a few footnotes as a basis for someone else to address their own particular needs."[21] The contributors to this book suggest that when Barth's theology is read in the South African crisis, the reader is *required* to address the challenges arising out of this context. In so doing we share in the process of reclaiming a corpus of literature that has not always been seen to be among the resources for the liberation of the oppressed.

Certainly it is the common opinion of critical theologians in South Africa that the power of Barth's theology never reached either the English-speaking or Afrikaans communities in South Africa, and that it has made little or no impact in the black community. Indeed, what Barthian thought has penetrated these communities has, with a few notable exceptions, been a sterile, ahistorical, and prescriptive dogma that has failed to address the most urgent contextual needs of the community. It has also failed to do justice to the context of crisis in which Barth was writing.

A generation of "conservative" teachers of theology have left their marks on the white Afrikaner community: A. B. du Preez, who taught systematic theology at the University of Pretoria for twenty-five years; F. J. M. Potgieter at the University of Stellenbosch; Ben Engelbrecht at the University of Pretoria; and S. P. van der Walt at Potchefstroom University. Each of these rejected Barth's theology for a variety of reasons, and apparently none of them fully understood the significance of its radical critique for their own thought—or perhaps they understood it too well! Exceptions in that formative generation of teachers include Johannes Lombard and J. A. (Lex) van Wyk, both of whom were students of Barth in Basel. The former was virtually driven out of the white Dutch Reformed Church but was responsible for establishing the Faculty of Theology at the University of South Africa. The latter spent virtually his entire life at the University of the North, teaching black students for the ministry in the Nederduitse Gereformeerde Kerk in Afrika. The most noted exception of that generation, however, is B. B. Keet, who taught systematic theology at Stellenbosch University until his retirement in the late sixties. He condemned apartheid as both biblically unjustifiable and untenable on practical grounds—in the face of the most zealous theological and political support for apartheid by his own church.[22] Then, in the centenary year of the Stellenbosch Seminary of the Nederduitse Gereformeerde Kerk, he reflected on a century of Reformed theology, insisting that Barth was a theologian his church could not afford to ignore.[23] Subsequent history would prove this point. Two years after the centenary lecture Keet prophetically said of the South African crisis what he implied of a theological heritage—"the bell has already tolled!"[24]

In English-speaking universities and seminaries Barth was scarcely taught for a variety of reasons. Some teachers of theology in these institutions failed to teach Barth's theology for the simple reason that his thought was not part of their own theological repertoire. In other cases Barth was suppressed out of a desire to protect a certain brand of Protestant "orthodoxy." Until recently theology was taught on only one English-language university campus, Rhodes University in Grahamstown. The chair in theology was instituted in 1947 and first held by Horton Davies, who showed no apparent interest in Barth. He was followed by N. H. G. Robinson, who had an extensive knowledge of Barth, but his stay was too short for this to make a significant impact. His successor, W. D. Maxwell, again showed little interest in Barth, while the present incumbent, Angus Holland, does have a detailed knowledge of Barth's writings. He has not, however, succeeded in inspiring many students to grasp the overt significance of Barth for the burning issues of South Africa today, nor has he sought to show the relevance of Barth to the South African situation in his own writings. This means that Barth continues to remain remote from the churches in this country. Yet, as already suggested, because of the dominant influence of Barth in the history of Protestant thought, there are at least some theologically trained preachers who have some acquaintance with Barth's thought, even if only through secondary sources.

Until recently, black theological training in South Africa has always been under the influence of white teachers, and the limited exposure to Barth in the white community has been carried over into black seminaries. In recent times, theological trends in the Federal Theological Seminary, the major center for training black ministers in South Africa, have been shaped by a mixture of traditional and African-contextual interests, and again the interest in Barth has been limited.

From Protestant Orthodoxy to False Piety

The contours of theological thought and teaching in South Africa are too complex to discuss in any detail. I have already suggested the central dichotomy in Afrikaner theology, founded as it is on two apparently conflicting theological approaches: Kuyperian theologized nationalism and an Andrew Murray style of pietism. What is becoming increasingly clear, however, is that both of these traditions have been appropriated to legitimate the existing order. And both misuse Barth's theology. In a study on the changing shape of religion in the South African context I have argued that

> the adherents of these two traditions have been able to live harmoniously together. When pietism becomes a form of other-worldly preoccupation, the political stage is left to the political theologians of patriotism. Yet, when the latter falter in their patriotism, or are unable to substantiate their position against conflicting political theologies, the secular guardians of the nation, eager for what religious legitimation they can muster, opt for a form of apolitical pietism . . . leaving politics to the secular forces of "national interest."[25]

When white patriotic theologians held full sway in Afrikaner theological circles, Barth's theology was used as an ingredient in the quest for "true belief" (and often found wanting) in the affirmation of "other-worldly" theological axioms. Yet, in recent times, some *verligte* Afrikaner theologians have turned away from old-style patriotic theology—suggesting that this kind of synthesis of nationalism and theology is little short of idolatrous.[26] This has, in some instances, led to a one-sided emphasis on Barth's sense of discontinuity between human strivings and divine purpose, to the neglect of Barth's divine critique of human political aspirations. The outcome is a form of false piety that leaves "the world without God and God without the world."[27] Politics are then indeed left to the secular forces of "national interest." The result is a kind of nineteenth-century Lutheran doctrine of the two kingdoms so decisively condemned by Barth.

Some theologians have failed to deal with the fundamental challenge of Barth's theology for South Africa. Others have ignored him. Still others have managed to appropriate his theology for the benefit of their own particular agendas. There are, however, few critical theologians who would deny the significance of Barth for a land torn apart by the absolutizing of conflicting ideologies. God's No to such absolutism is the beginning of God's Yes to the possibility of a society within which humanity's God-given freedom becomes a reality.

Paradigms of Radical Grace

Dirkie Smit

> Looking back, we may well ask with amazement how it was that the Reformation, and . . . the whole of earlier and especially more recent Protestantism . . . could overlook this dimension of the Gospel which is so clearly attested in the New Testament. . . . (Barth, *CD* IV/2, 233)

In Protestant circles in South Africa, and especially in the churches of the Dutch Reformed Church family, the conviction that "God is the God of the poor," or that "God is on the side of the oppressed," or that "God is in a special way the God of the destitute" is regarded as controversial.[1] Many people, including ministers of religion, find this claim difficult to accept. Even people who reject apartheid wholeheartedly feel uneasy about this kind of statement concerning God.

The reasons for this controversial quality and uneasiness are manifold. To some, the Bible and the Christian tradition has simply never taught this "option for the poor." To some, this claim fundamentally contradicts their understanding of the obvious universality of God's love and actions according to the Bible, especially the New Testament. To some, the idea of partiality is alien to their own moral convictions and not applicable to God. To some, it suggests a parallel of the very idea they are rejecting in Afrikaner civil religion, namely, the particularistic claim to be an *uitverkore volk,* an elected nation. To some, it sounds like nothing more than a crude theological restatement of Marxism and class-struggle theory. To others, the ends to which such an expression can be turned within the ideological discourse taking place in South African society at present seems unacceptable. They fear that it may become a mere ideological weapon, used to give religious sanction or legitimation to all kinds of inhuman and, to their mind, un-Christian actions, without providing a way of distinguishing among these activities.[2]

It is impossible to deal here in any detail with these controversial points of view. A crucially important factor, however, is that—apart

17

from all the other elements involved—a typical feature of the legacy of Protestantism in general, and the type of Reformed Protestantism influential in South Africa in particular, makes it difficult for people born and bred in this tradition to accept this claim without hesitation.

Although in principle it is possible to describe a particular religious community in terms of its social construct of reality, to do so in practice is a very difficult task. There have been attempts to describe the typical features of a particular religious community from different angles. Since Troeltsch and Weber, Christian communities have often been described in terms of their so-called ethic and the way they acted economically, politically, or socially. Other attempts frequently have been made to typify different kinds of spirituality or to distinguish between traditions or groups on a number of different scores. In each of these attempts, an important aspect may indeed be highlighted.[3]

This is a fruitful reminder that doctrinal differences between confessional groups may not be, and indeed often are not, the most important issues involved. Any attempt, therefore, to describe a particular group in terms of its convictions and doctrines alone runs the risk of giving a distorted picture.[4] Several such attempts, from different angles, have already been made to characterize some of the branches of Reformed Protestantism in South Africa.[5] But a comprehensive account is still lacking.[6]

Keeping all this in mind, it is still true that one essential feature of Protestantism in general—and definitely of the Dutch Reformed Protestantism that exists in South Africa—is the confession of the centrality of justification by grace alone: the justification of the sinner by faith. This doctrine is often regarded as typically Lutheran; traditionally, Lutherans themselves see it as the *articulus stantis et cadentis ecclesiae* . . . (the article by which the church stands or falls).[7] But it is an emphasis that permeates Protestant theology and spirituality in general.

To be strictly accurate, this doctrine is not only a doctrine—in fact, it is not even primarily a doctrine. It describes rather the comprehensive vision of Protestantism: its spirituality, its way of life, its most basic affirmation. It penetrates and influences all aspects of Protestant life and thought and clearly colors all the doctrinal loci. The central religious, even human, problem is the problem of sin and forgiveness, which in turn means that this view dominates Protestant anthropology. The purpose of the Christ-event is seen as God's will to save (some) from sin.[8] The nature of the church, its membership, its calling, and its ministry can be understood only in terms of this central emphasis.[9] Faith, the sacraments, salvation, eschatology, and the Christian life are all defined in terms of this basic conviction. Justification by grace alone becomes the overriding religious perspective.

It would be fruitful, space permitting, to look at the particular way in which these motifs of the justification of the sinner and the forgiveness of sins have been understood in Dutch Reformed circles in South Africa. The strong influence of Scottish pietism, for example, has clearly stamped the understanding of this doctrine to a very large degree. But while such a detailed analysis would certainly help to enforce our argument, even without it the thesis still applies to Protestantism in general.

Barth on Reconciliation

In treating the miracles of Jesus, Barth makes a very relevant comment. He writes:

> Looking back, we may well ask with amazement how it was that the Reformation, and (apart from a few exceptions) the whole of earlier and especially more recent Protestantism as it followed both Luther and Calvin, could overlook this dimension of the Gospel which is so clearly attested in the New Testament—its power as a message of mercifully omnipotent and unconditionally complete liberation from *phthora*, death and wrong as the power of evil. How could Protestantism as a whole, only too faithful to Augustine, the "father of the West," orientate itself in a way which was so one-sidedly anthropological (by the problem of repentance instead of by its presupposition—the kingdom of God)? In other words, how could it become such a moralistic affair—so dull, so indifferent to the question of man himself, and therefore so lacking in joy? How could it possibly overlook the fact that it was depriving even its specific doctrine of justification and sanctification of so radiant a basis and confirmation by not looking very differently at the character of the self-revelation of God in the Son of Man as it emerges in the miracles of Jesus, in these works of God; by not considering the freedom of the grace which appeared in Him? And in spite of its many saints and their many miracles, there is nothing much to be learned in this respect from Western Catholicism. . . . From the Reformers we can at least know what free grace might be, and therefore learn, perhaps, to recognise its radicalism as revealed in the miracles of Jesus. But where the Reformers were opposed and the doctrine of free grace completely rejected, it seems that an almost hopeless barrier was set up to any advance in this direction. (*CD* IV/2, 233)

Although this particular aspect of Barth's work has received almost no attention in the secondary literature, it reflects ideas fundamentally important to Barth himself and very relevant to our present situation. In order to understand the detail of this quotation, however, it is necessary to view it in a broader context. Barth's work is such a close-knit unity that one can understand any particular part only by approaching it from the outside, as though through layers of concentric circles, and by constantly reckoning with the rest of Barth's exposition. Unfortunately, this is only too often not done, especially by people trying to find "juicy expressions"—of which there are many!—for their own purposes, without much respect for the original argument.

We are, therefore, first going to consider Barth's treatment of the doctrine of reconciliation itself as the outer circle, then examine the paragraph on "the Royal Man" in which he makes this comment, and then look at his discussion of the miracles, which forms the immediate context, before returning to this quotation itself.

Volume IV of the *Church Dogmatics* deals, of course, with the doctrine of reconciliation. Reduced to its simplest form, reconciliation means God with us (IV/1, 3-21). What does that mean? It is not simply a concept, an idea, a sign, or a symbol; it is rather reality, history, borne out in "the bearer of this name," that is, in Jesus Christ.

Accordingly, it is correct to say that the whole doctrine of reconciliation deals primarily with God and with God's work. Because of this, the doctrine of reconciliation is also primarily about Jesus Christ. To speak about God and his work is, for Barth, to speak about Jesus Christ. There is no other way of knowing God, as he has argued so powerfully in the preceding volumes of the *Church Dogmatics*.[10] Volume IV therefore contains Barth's explicit Christology, although for him in a very definite sense all theology is Christology.

The whole of Volume IV is subdivided into three major parts on Jesus Christ: "the Lord as Servant," dealing with the fulfillment of the priestly work (IV/1); "the Servant as Lord," dealing with the fulfillment of the kingly work (IV/2); and "the true Witness" (both volumes of IV/3) dealing with the fulfillment of the prophetic work. As was the case with the other doctrines, a further volume on the special ethics based on this doctrine of reconciliation ought to have followed, but he never completed this and only a fragment was published (IV/4 Fragment). Since then, the surviving draft that, if completed, would have formed the special ethics of reconciliation (*CD* IV/4) was published under the title *The Christian Life: Lecture Fragments.*

Because it is all about Jesus Christ, the doctrine of reconciliation is also for Barth primarily about God's act of grace. Everything hinges on God's own merciful and effective act wherein his grace is his free turning to humanity (IV/1, 79-92). Unconditionally, and under no constraint to do so, God turns freely and mercifully to humanity. In so doing, God crosses the frontiers, both of his own glory and of human sin, and fulfills the broken covenant on which creation itself was based. God, mercifully and freely, thus creates and grounds a new human subject.

> The formula "God everything and man nothing" as a description of grace is not merely a "shocking simplification" but complete nonsense. Man is nothing . . . without the grace of God. . . . In the giving of His Son, however, in reconciling the world to Himself in Christ, God is indeed everything but only in order that man may not be nothing. . . . The meaning and purpose of the atonement made in Jesus Christ is that man . . . should be maintained, or rather, newly created and grounded, from above. . . . This creating and grounding of a human subject . . . is, in fact, the event of the atonement. (IV/1, 89)

In short, because of this completely free act of God's grace in Jesus Christ to be "with us," the doctrine of reconciliation is, in a secondary sense, also about the new human subject that is thereby constituted and called with a vocation to respond to God's act of grace.

This new human subject is reconstituted through the Holy Spirit. The Holy Spirit effects the reconciliation in the Christian community as well as in the individual. The Holy Spirit gathers together, builds up, and sends forth the community, establishing the individual in faith, love, and hope.

The contents of Barth's doctrine of reconciliation can therefore be divided in a sketch as in that on p. 22. This larger context is very important in understanding the particulars of what Barth is saying because of the intricate way in which his thoughts are interrelated and continuously presuppose one another.

Barth on "the Royal Man"

Within this doctrine of reconciliation, Barth discusses the miracles (*CD* IV/2) when he deals with Jesus as "the Royal Man." He is therefore describing Jesus in his kingly work as "very man exalted and reconciled." He is interested in the historical figure of Jesus as presented in the Gospels.

In the "preface" Barth explicitly points out the importance of this particular christological section, which deals with the humanity of

THE CONTENT OF THE DOCTRINE OF RECONCILIATION IN BARTH

The Work of God the Reconciler

The Grace of God in Jesus Christ

Jesus Christ the Lord as Servant

1. Obedience of the Son of God
2. Pride and fall of humanity
3. Justification of humanity
4. The Holy Spirit and the gathering of the Christian community
5. The Holy Spirit and faith

Jesus Christ the Servant as Lord

1. Exaltation of the Son of Man
2. Sloth and misery of humankind
3. Sanctification of humankind
4. The Holy Spirit and the building up of the Christian community
5. The Holy Spirit and love

Jesus Christ the True Witness

1. Glory of the Mediator, and the falsehood and condemnation of humanity
2. The vocation of humanity
3. The Holy Spirit and the sending of the Christian community
4. The Holy Spirit and hope

Jesus Christ. "For it is there," he notes, "that the decisions are made. There is no legitimate way to an understanding of the Christian life other than that which we enter here." It is important to keep this in mind.

What does he say about Jesus in this particular subsection on "the Royal Man"? In other words, how does the New Testament tradition present Jesus "as a man among the men of His time," according to Barth? His description contains four main points, the second of which we shall deal with in detail.

First, he points to the distinctiveness of Jesus' presence. He was present in a way which could not fail to be seen or heard. He was unforgettably unique. He demanded decisions through his encounters with others. He was, and he made, history.

The second section becomes very important for the present purpose. The Jesus of the Gospels, as a man, "exists analogously to the mode of existence of God." The term *analogously* is especially important. "In what He thinks and wills and does, in His attitude, there is a correspondence, a parallel in the creaturely world, to the plan and purpose and work and attitude of God."

The fact that this royal man, Jesus, is a reflection of God in correspondence with God's own purpose and work can be deduced from four important observations:

First, "the royal man shares as such the strange destiny which falls on God in His people and the world—to be the One who is ignored and forgotten and despised and discounted by men." Barth then goes on in a forceful manner to explain this humiliation of Jesus. He adds that, although this fact is often stated, "its inevitability is not always grasped." It was inevitable because it pleased Jesus, despite being, or better, precisely being the royal man, to share "the lot of God in the world which had fallen away from Him."

Second, "almost to the point of prejudice," as Barth puts it, he ignored all those who are high and mighty and wealthy in the world in favor of the weak and meek and lowly. Barth then demonstrates how Jesus did this in different spheres.

> He did this even in the moral sphere, ignoring the just for sinners, and in the spiritual sphere, finally ignoring Israel for the Gentiles. . . . Throughout the New Testament the kingdom of God, the Gospel and the man Jesus have a remarkable affinity, which is no mere egalitarianism, to all those who are in the shadows as far as concerns what men estimate to be fortune and possessions and success and even fellowship with God. . . . One reason is the distinctive solidarity of the man Jesus with the God who in the eyes of the world—and not merely the

ordinary world, but the moral and spiritual world as well—is also poor in this way, existing . . . somewhere on the margin in its scale of values, at an unimportant level. . . . In fellowship and conformity with this God who is poor in the world the royal man Jesus is also poor, and fulfills this transvaluation of all values, acknowledging those who (without necessarily being better) are in different ways poor men as this world counts poverty.

The three qualifications in the last sentence are all crucially important. It is in analogy, in correspondence, in fellowship or conformity with the God who is poor and humiliated in this world that Jesus is poor and humiliated. In so doing he acknowledges, joins, loves, and helps those who are not necessarily "better" in any way. The reason for his solidarity with them is precisely *not* based on their merits or superior qualities, but on his solidarity with the God of grace and free, unconditional mercy. And, finally, he thereby acknowledges people who are poor in different ways: economic, material poverty is most definitely included, but so also are spiritual and moral poverty. As a matter of fact, Barth explicitly calls any restriction of this solidarity to poverty "in a purely economic sense . . . a softening" of the truth of the Gospels, to be rejected together with any "softening" of the "starkness" with which the economically deprived are unmistakably also included and addressed.

Third, the conformity of Jesus with the mode of existence and attitude of God consists in "the pronouncedly revolutionary character of His relationship to the orders of life and value current in the world around Him." Barth explains:

> Jesus was not in any sense a reformer championing new orders against the old ones, contesting the latter in order to replace them by the former. He did not range Himself and His disciples with any of the existing parties. . . . Jesus did not identify Himself with them. Nor did He set up against them an opposing party. He did not represent or defend or champion any programme—whether political, economic, moral or religious, whether conservative or progressive. He was equally suspected and disliked by the representatives of all such programmes, although He did not particularly attack any of them. Why His existence was so unsettling on every side was that He set all programmes and principles in question.

And why could Jesus do that?

> He enjoyed and displayed . . . a remarkable freedom which again we can only describe as royal. He had need of none of [these orders]. . . . On the other hand, he had no need consistently to break any of them,

to try to overthrow them altogether, to work for their replacement or amendment. He could live in these orders. . . . He simply revealed the limit and frontier of all these things—the freedom of the kingdom of God. He simply existed in freedom and summoned others to it. . . . Inevitably, then, he clashed with these orders. . . . But it was not these incidental disclosures of the freedom of God which made Him a revolutionary far more radical than any that came either before or after Him. It was the freedom itself. . . . In the last resort, it was again conformity with God Himself which constituted the secret of the character of Jesus on this side too.

When Barth explains this in more detail from the biblical material, he points first of all to "the passive conservatism of Jesus," but then to the "superiority, the freedom of the kingdom of God," which established "a crisis," a "radical and indissoluble antithesis" between the kingdom of God and all human kingdoms. Again, in this freedom Jesus lives in correspondence with God himself.

The truth of all our knowledge of God is at stake in these descriptions.

That is why we have first had to set Jesus against man and his cosmos as the poor man who if He blessed and befriended any blessed and befriended the poor and not the rich, the incomparable revolutionary who laid the axe at the root of the trees, who pitilessly exposed the darkness of human order in the cosmos, questioning it in a way which is quite beyond our capacity to answer. We do not know God at all if we do not know Him as the One who is absolutely opposed to our whole world which has fallen away from Him. . . . If we think we know Him in any other way, what we really know is only the world itself, ourselves. . . . In the man Jesus, God has separated Himself from this misinterpretation. . . . But again, we do not really know Jesus (the Jesus of the New Testament) if we do not know Him as this poor man, as this (if we may risk the dangerous word) partisan of the poor, and finally as this revolutionary.

But then he adds—and this remark is crucially important—"this certainly cannot be our last word."

Last, and this is by far the most important aspect for Barth, Jesus, "like God Himself, is not against men but for men—even for men in all the impossibility of their perversion." This is the decisive point, says Barth. Jesus is also, and ultimately, the reflection of God's divine Yes.

The man Jesus is the royal man in the fact that He is not merely one man with others but *the* man for them (as God is for them), the man in whom the love and faithfulness and salvation and glory of God are addressed to [men] . . . in spite of their form . . . in spite of their own estrangement and fundamental error . . . in spite of their attempted safeguards . . . in spite of the misery to which they necessarily fall victim in this estrangement and error. . . .

This line of thought is extremely relevant to our question. Barth adds:

The divine Yes echoed by the royal man Jesus is the divine Word of comfort for this very misery, and only as such, and working back from it, for the human corruption which is the basis for it. God grapples with sin as He has mercy on the men who suffer in this way as sinners.

When he later deals with the miracles, Barth will again draw on these ideas. And in the following paragraph 65 he describes the human condition of need under the two headings of "the sloth of man" and "the misery of man." Together they constitute the human condition in which the royal man finds humanity.

The point here is that Jesus lives his life for humanity as Savior and not as Judge, and in that he reflects the divine Yes to humanity, especially humanity in suffering and misery. Barth deals extensively with the joy that Jesus brought, with the *Magnificat* and the *Benedictus,* with Jesus' compassion on the crowd, and with the beatitudes. In all of these Jesus is the royal man, "the supreme and most proper image of the invisible God."

To summarize, then, this second section: Jesus reflects God in that he shares God's rejection, in that he transvaluates all values by favoring the weak and humble and not the high and mighty, in that he approaches all human orders with the revolutionary divine freedom that cuts across all human parties and programs. Most especially, he lives for human beings and not against them, and in so doing he echoes God's fundamental Yes.

In the third section, Barth tries to understand Jesus in his life-act, that is, in the interrelatedness of his words and works. He deals first with the words of Jesus and then with his works or miracles.

The fourth and final section is again extremely important, for it provides the ultimate key to understanding the humanity of Jesus, this Servant as Lord in his kingly work. In this section Barth discusses the death of Jesus on the cross. The cross is no alien element in this royal life. As a matter of fact, everything that has been said thus far is shaped and determined by the cross. There Jesus, the royal man, receives his coronation. The cross is neither tragic nor a mishap. It does not spell despair, but triumph.

Barth discusses the predictions of the passion, the positive interpretation of the cross in the fourth Gospel, and Paul's view. The pre-Easter Jesus expected the cross and moved toward it voluntarily, in fulfillment of the divine predetermination. This means that there is a cross for the disciples as well. They no longer stand in the shadow of Jesus' cross, because his cross spells for them "light and power and glory and promise and fulfillment, present liberation and the hope of that which is still to come, the forgiveness of sins, and here and now eternal life." But they do stand under the "sign and direction" of his cross. The divine "must" of his passion is extended to them also.

This difference is important. The cross of the disciples

> is not the cross of Christ. This has been carried once and for all, and does not need to be carried again. There can be no question of identification with Him, of a repetition of His suffering and death. But it is a matter of each Christian carrying his own individual cross. . . . This is not the primary *theologia crucis* of the Gospels, but it is certainly the secondary. . . . It must not be equated or confused with the primary *theologia crucis,* which is wholly and exclusively that of the cross of Jesus, but it cannot and must not be separated from it.

In the secondary literature it has often and quite correctly been emphasized that the cross provides the real key to understanding Barth's view of Jesus.[11] Any interpretation of Barth's view of the humanity of Jesus and of his unconditional solidarity with humanity in misery that does not take seriously the cross and the divine "must" is a fatal misunderstanding of Barth. Any interpretation, therefore, that does not distinguish clearly between what Barth calls "the primary *theologia crucis* of the Gospels," the good news of the triumph of God over the powers in the cross of Jesus, and "the secondary *theologia crucis* of the Gospels," the cross of the disciples, also misrepresents Barth.

Barth on the Miracles

Within this broader context it is now possible to look very specifically at how Barth understands the miracles of Jesus.

The works of Jesus always accompany his words. In fact, his word makes cosmic history on this earth, in space and time, by the lake and in the towns of Galilee, in Jerusalem and on the way to it, in the circumstances of specific individuals, as well as in the activities or works of Jesus. These works are the light of truth kindling his speech into actuality. They are the demonstration of the identity of his proclamation of the kingdom of God, the Lordship of God, the divine *coup d'état,* with the event itself. The will of God is being done on earth as it is done in heaven. The rule of God takes place in the sight of believers and unbelievers. His activity is always the preaching of the gospel, teaching, and proclamation, but now in a cosmic form. It is always "the revelation of the decision which has been made in the fact of his human existence among other men." The Gospels and the tradition did not think it worthwhile to give an account of any other activities of Jesus. What was of interest was not incidental biographical detail that could make him a more human figure to us, but solely those acts in which the kingdom itself was proclaimed and realized in time and space.

These acts are therefore different from the actions of other human beings and indicate the presence of an extraordinary reality. They represent something completely new in face of the usual order, form, and development of life. That is why they can only be understood by those who have the necessary ears and eyes as signs of the kingdom drawn near. They display a paradoxical character. In them an alien will and an unknown power invaded the general course of things in what the majority of human beings accept as self-evident and inflexible normalcy. The customary order was breached by an incursion, the possibility of which they were not able to explain. Therefore, these acts caused astonishment, amazement, opposition, and fear.

His acts also differed from other accounts of miracles from human history. Barth points to a list of important differences, two of which are very relevant to our discussion.

> The miracles of Jesus do not take place in the sphere or as the content of even a partial attempt at the amelioration of world-conditions or as an organised improvement of the human lot. Jesus was not in any sense an activist. As we shall see, his miracles followed a very definite line. But it was not the line of a welfare-programme executed with the assistance of supernatural powers. . . .
>
> How gladly we would learn of a continuation, of definite and lasting results, of His beneficent activity. But the Gospels have nothing to tell us along these lines. His well-doing never became an institution. . . .

Barth adds that the miracles of Jesus do have a "transparent character," a "symbolic quality"; they are also parables. Not only are they concrete history but they also serve as models or originals of

> certain situations in the history of the development and being and formation and work of the community which in His discipleship is charged with the continued proclamation of the Gospel, the kingdom and His own name. . . .

The fathers were very conscious of this, and for that reason they were at this point far better exegetes than those who, in a panic-stricken fear of what is condemned root and branch as "allegorising," refuse to look in this direction at all.

Both these ideas, that the miracles are fundamentally different from any kind of activism, and that they are parables or models and not only historical actions, will have to be taken into serious account when one tries to understand the implications of the miracles for Barth.

Now we come to the core of the argument. Barth explicitly asks: "But what is this kingdom of God, and what do we mean when we say that they were miracles of this kingdom?" To answer this question, he examines in great detail the nature of the miracles. They are, of course, acts of divine power, but such a description is not precise enough. One must try to understand the nature of this power. Barth frames the crucial question in a very interesting way: "We have to ask what it means that they took place unconditionally and are thus characterised as inconceivable." In other words, it is precisely their unconditional character that makes them inconceivable or miraculous to the eyes and minds of human beings, caught in what are generally accepted as conceivable or normal actions. Barth says that "a completely new and astonishing light" is cast on the human situation in and with these works of Jesus. This "light" running through all the accounts shows these works to be signs of the kingdom. What is this "light," then? Barth discusses five characteristics, all of them directly bearing on our question.

First, he asks about the kind of human being to whom Jesus turns in these works.

> The answer is obvious. It is the man with whom things are going badly; who is needy and frightened and harassed. . . . The picture brought before us is that of suffering. . . .
>
> We may turn away from this aspect of human existence. We may close our eyes to it. We may argue that human life as a whole is not really like a great hospital. But apart from this aspect the miracles of Jesus cannot be brought into proper focus and genuinely seen and understood. For human life as it emerges in this activity of Jesus is really like a great hospital whose many departments in some way enfold us all.

He expands on the last comment.

> The theme is that of human suffering, in which the distinctions between smaller and greater degrees of painfulness are of no decisive

29

> importance, the apparently slighter evil being often the greatest, and
> man being always a poor man for whom things go badly even when he
> is not actually *in extremis.*

In short, "His action is always in response to human misery."

Second, this suffering is primarily physical suffering. The
miracles address "almost exclusively [this] 'natural' existence in the
narrower sense, [this] physical existence." Man becomes a prisoner as
he is subjected to suffering in this sphere, and "that is the problem of
the miracles of Jesus."

> His miraculous action to man is to free him from this prison. . . . He
> unburdens man; He releases him.
> He can be man again—a whole man in the elemental sense. His
> existence as a creature in the natural cosmos is normalised. We must
> not ignore or expunge the phrase—as a creature in the natural cosmos.
> It is as such that he is radically blessed in the miracles of Jesus.

Barth feels the need to accentuate this polemically against the
popular interpretation of the miracles. He points to the "remarkable
and almost offensive feature . . . which has been continuously obscured," that is, painted over in ethical colors, in so much well-meaning exposition (especially in the Western church). What is that?

> In these stories it does not seem to be of any great account that the men
> who suffer as creatures are above all sinful men, men who are at fault
> in relation to God, their neighbours and themselves, who are therefore
> guilty and have betrayed themselves into all kinds of trouble.
> No, the important thing in these stories is not that they are sinners
> but that they are sufferers.

He argues that the term *soozesthai* ("saved") in the miracle sto-
ries "has nothing whatever to do, directly, with the conversion of the
'saved.'"

> Jesus does not first look at their past, and then at their tragic present in
> the light of it. But from their present He creates for them a new future.
> He does not ask, therefore, concerning their sin. . . . The help and
> blessing that He brings are quite irrespective of their sin.

And then he adds: "He acts almost (indeed exactly) in the same way
as His Father in heaven."

Third, the God whose power is active in the miracles is the God
who is always directly interested in humanity as his creatures.

> Beyond or above or through his sin He is interested in man him-
> self. . . . He is interested in him as this specific cosmic being. He has

not forgotten him or left him to himself. In spite of his sin He has not given him up. He maintains His covenant with him. . . .

He takes his sin seriously. But He takes even more seriously, with a primary seriousness, the fact that he is His man even as a sinner and above all that He is the God even of this sinful man.

In short, God is not interested in human beings *because* of their sin but in spite of their sin, *because* he is God and they are his creatures and therefore part of his covenant. And the miracles demonstrate this most powerfully, since they take

the form of this direct comforting of the sad, this free liberation of the poor, these benefits which come so unconditionally to man; when in this form [God's serious interest] consists quite simply in the fact that oppressed and therefore anxious and harassed men can breathe and live again, can again be men.

Fourth, in the miracles God self-evidently places himself at the side of humanity, makes their suffering his own, and takes up their struggle against the hostile powers.

That which causes suffering to man as His creatures is also and above all painful and alien and antithetical to Himself. . . . God does not will that which troubles and torments and disturbs and destroys man. He does not will the entanglement and humiliation and distress and shame. . . . He does not will the destruction of man, but his salvation. And he wills this in the basic and elemental sense that he should be whole. . . .

The sorrow which openly or secretly fills the heart of man is primarily in the heart of God. The shame which comes on man is primarily a violation of His own glory. The enemy who does not let man breathe and live, harrassing him with fear and pain, is primarily His enemy. . . .

God Himself engages the nothingness which aims to destroy man. . . .

And the coming of His Kingdom, His seizure of power on earth, is centrally and decisively the power and revelation of the contradiction and opposition in which, speaking and acting in His own cause, He takes the side of man and enters the field against this power of destruction in all its forms. That is why the activity of the Son of Man . . . necessarily has the crucial and decisive form of liberation, redemption, restoration, normalisation.

In his discussion of the biblical material, Barth pays special attention to the exorcisms of Jesus. He calls them "quite clearly military actions." Jesus' activities are "a defiance of the power of destruction which enslaves humanity, of *phthora* in all its forms."

And then Barth makes use of some noteworthy expressions. The miracles "are not a neutral force or omnipotence, but the omnipotence of mercy, an active mercy, hostile to the powers on behalf of humanity." This is what we must deal with in the miracles, and precisely because we must deal with it they are miracles! "For what is miraculous and new and incomprehensible in them . . . is that God is a God who for man's sake cannot stand aside in this matter, who cannot rest. . . ."

Last, he wants to "emphasize and underline again" something that he has already mentioned but that needs separate underscoring because it is so decisive. It is gloriously free grace that is active in the miracles. That is the sole motivation; the sin of humanity is no condition at all.

> We have seen that the fact that man is a sinner . . . is not taken into account. . . . The whole perversion of the heart and attitude of man emerges here and there on the margin, but only on the extreme margin. From what we are told of Him, Jesus is not really concerned with what from the anthropological point of view is the cause of human misery, but only with the misery itself and as such. In these passages it is not at the side of the bad man but the suffering man that He, God Himself, sets Himself. It is to the help of the sufferer that He comes. And that He does so is quite undeserved by him, the creature. . . .
>
> It is simply and exclusively because this is the good will of God for him.

Barth on Unconditional and Radical Free Grace

We have now returned to the remarkable quotation with which we started. It is precisely at this point that Barth expresses his amazement that Protestantism has largely failed to see this dimension in the gospel that is so clearly attested to in the New Testament.

What is this dimension? That the message of the kingdom, symbolically enacted in the miracles of Jesus, is a message of the omnipotence of mercy and unconditionally complete liberation from the destructive powers of evil.

Why did Protestantism overlook it? Because, following a traditional reading of Augustine, Protestants have oriented themselves to a particular bias. They understood the message from the viewpoint of humanity—humanity as sinful and in need of repentance and forgiveness—instead of from the viewpoint of the kingdom itself, of God and his unconditional, free grace toward humanity, not only as sinners, but as his creatures in need of total redemption and a new life.

As a result of that bias, Protestantism became a "moralistic affair" and, remarkably, "so indifferent to the question of man itself," that question of humanity in misery and suffering. Paradoxically, with that emphasis Protestantism deprived this central doctrine of justification and sanctification of its "radiant" basis in the freedom of grace that was so powerfully demonstrated in the miracles. By looking at the gospel from an anthropological perspective, the sin of humanity was virtually made a new condition for grace! The only way, and the only reason why, God could be believed to show mercy toward someone was because of that person's sin and guilt. Sin became almost meritorious, therefore restricting God's free and unlimited grace.

Thus, Protestantism lost the radicalism of free grace as revealed in Jesus' miracles. Consequently, traditional expositions tried to reinterpet these miracle-stories into "ethical colors." And, of course, where Western Catholicism opposed the Reformers and rejected the doctrine of free grace, "almost hopeless barriers" were set up.

In short, according to Barth, the miracles help us to understand God's grace in its radicality and unconditionality, addressed to humanity in sloth and misery—not only to sinners, but to God's creatures, the partners in the covenant, in sin and in suffering as a result of the power of evil. In the act of reconciliation in Christ, God overcomes all these barriers in his free grace and his omnipotent mercy. That is the message and reality of the kingdom, the heart of the gospel, the content of all theology, the reason for abundant joy.

As we have seen, this particular discussion occupies a central place in Barth's doctrine of reconciliation, his Christology, and therefore in the *Church Dogmatics* as a whole. These ideas also play an important role in other writings by Barth from the same period. Of special relevance would be "The Gift of Freedom" and "The Humanity of God."[12]

A Paradigm of God's Grace

Perhaps a very apt way of describing Barth's position in this regard is to use an expression coined by Durand, and to call the miracles *"a paradigm of God's grace."*

Durand uses this expression when he deals with the theme of God and suffering. In referring to biblical material, he comments that one cannot simply ignore the conviction that God is for the poor and oppressed. It might have been possible to reject this simply as a case of ideological language within theology were it not for the over-whelming evidence provided by the biblical tradition itself. Durand draws attention to several of these strands of tradition and concludes that they are not accidental opinions that can be ignored while retaining the gospel itself. No, the whole gospel emphasizes the special way in which God cares for the poor, the oppressed, and the lowly, because the gospel itself is "God's turning in grace towards human beings not able to help themselves. Accordingly, God's merciful care for the poor and the oppressed in their misery becomes a paradigm of his grace." He further points out that precisely because this is a paradigm of grace, the church must be careful not to stereotype it into an ideology by claiming God's support only for specific people or groups over against other people or groups. Then we would once again lose sight of the free and unconditional nature of grace.[13]

This expression, "paradigm of grace," therefore makes it possible to see the miracles as yet another illustration, albeit an extremely important one, of God's grace, God's will, God's mercy, and God's heart also attested to by several other trajectories of tradition in the Bible.[14]

This interpretation is in line with Berkouwer's interpretation of Barth's theology in his famous *The Triumph of Grace in the Theology of Karl Barth*.[15] It is well known by now that Barth, although appreciative of this interpretation of his theology, objected to the title because he was afraid that it could draw attention away from the *person* of Jesus Christ to an abstract *principle* of grace. In one of his last public talks, a radio broadcast commenting on Mozart's music, he repeated the same idea once again.[16] Not grace, but Jesus Christ: in Jesus Christ is grace.

With this understanding we are able to evaluate Carl Braaten's criticism of the theology of liberation, which is very relevant to our discussion. It is necessary to quote Braaten at length:

> Liberation theology is currently proposing a new paradigm of salvation. It is timely and appealing, but I wonder if it is sufficiently cogent and convincing. Liberation theology is right to focus on the wretchedness of the human condition, although it has in mind chiefly the misery of the poor and the oppressed. Liberation theology is right to work for the overthrow of all systems of domination which exploit and enslave people, although it tends to look through the narrow peephole of the class conflict in society. Liberation theology is right to call for the transformation of society and not to tolerate the situation of injustice, poverty, and oppression generated by the social system, although its rhetoric of denunciation, as with the prophets of Israel, is more clear

than its alternative vision of the new. But what do the liberation movements of whatever ilk, that promise to change the world for the better, have to do with the salvation which Christianity announces in the name of God's gospel about Jesus' cross and resurrection?

The kind of salvation that liberation theology lifts up is generally something Athens could in principle discover without the help of Jerusalem, something Marx in effect called for without reference to Jesus, something which will come about through human praxis without any dependence on God's act in Christ. This is its advantage, because it does not require Christians for its success. In light of Marx's idea of praxis, which liberation theologians use as a tool for analysis, the notion of God's saving act in Christ is, strictly speaking, bound to be viewed as a fetish. Praxis means a new course for action to change the world. Salvation awaits the outcome. Meanwhile there is only the class conflict. The call for conversion is now the call to join the struggle on the left side. The Christian is free to do this, of course. It is then a practical ethical decision which falls under Luther's rubric, *pecca fortiter*. It most certainly does not constitute what Christian faith means by *soteria*.

Liberation theology has made an option for socialistic salvation which shares the classical liberal vision of a society built on the principles of freedom and justice, and finally a society in which no group or class is dominated and oppressed by others. . . . The Christian hope of salvation is deeply suspicious of all political promises—from the left or the right or the middle—to inaugurate a world of freedom, peace, and justice. . . .

The liberationist idea of praxis is very seductive. Since Christian salvation *sola gratia* has failed to change the world, why not try a new approach—not faith, but praxis? Why leave it to God and do nothing?

I believe the soteriological deficit in the liberationist paradigm of salvation coincides with the turn away from Paul in contemporary theology and back to the historical Jesus. Paul stands for a soteriology that is oriented to the cross and resurrection of Jesus, whereas Jesus stands for the kingdom of God, which has only to be de-eschatologized, and particularly de-apocalypticized, to make it fit a this-worldly, inner-historical, socio-ethical interpretation of the gospel. . . .

Paul's message centered in justification through faith apart from the works of the law. . . . Justification through faith was at the heart of Paul's gospel. This was the view of the Reformers, and I believe they were basically right.[17]

The interesting aspect here is that Braaten also uses the category of paradigm and locates the difficulty of liberation theology in its "new" paradigm of salvation, oriented to the Jesus of the gospels rather than around Paul and the message of justification through faith.

I would suggest that Braaten is setting up false oppositions, and that by contradicting what need not be contradicted he is forced into alternatives that are neither convincing nor biblical. Is the choice really between acting or leaving everything to God and doing nothing? Is the choice really between Paul and Jesus? Do our ethical and political decisions really have nothing to do with our faith, only with "sinning boldly"? It would seem that beginning with a particular "paradigm of salvation," from an anthropological starting point, inevitably leads to such false alternatives.

Perhaps Durand's proposition is more helpful since he works not with a paradigm of salvation but with a paradigm of grace. In other words, can we not begin our reflection from what God has done in Jesus Christ, with his act of grace, with the message of the kingdom, and in that way try to take seriously Paul and the gospels, justification and liberation, sin and misery, poverty and oppression?

Ethical Implications Considered

Of course, an important question remains as to whether this conviction also has ethical implications, and if so, what are they? Is this confession concerning God's grace in Jesus Christ doxological only, or also ethical? What about Barth's warning that the miracles have nothing to do with activism and with the organized improvement of the human lot or world conditions? Does it follow that, because God in his unconditional and radical free grace is in a special way the God of the poor, the oppressed, and the destitute, the church must follow him and be "a church for the poor"? Are the poor then God's true church, and must the church "take the side of the poor"? What could all these expressions mean in concrete, ethical terms? These implications are manifold and extremely important for the life of the church today, especially in South Africa.

While it is impossible to attempt any definitive answers here, I would like to make some comments on the way we might ascertain Barth's own position on this question. To do so we will have to search for clues through the concentric circles of Barth's themes once again, this time from the inner to the outer circles.

In the immediate context itself, Barth gives no direct indication that he is dealing with our responsibility or possible reaction to God's offer of grace; he is only proclaiming God's grace in Jesus Christ. In fact, Barth deals extensively with faith as an adequate response. He distinguishes between those "who move towards the action of Jesus as those who are absolutely needy and poor and suffering and in misery" and *their* faith, and people "who come already from the place to which the others are only moving; those who have already received, who are already liberated and delivered, who see where they were blind," and *their* faith. Barth stresses the new freedom of the latter group as the key category to describe what faith brings to them. "These acts have not taken place for them in vain if . . . the Liberator has not merely restored to them their eyes or ears or members or reason, but . . . has given them the completely new freedom to believe in Him and in the God active and revealed in Him." More explicitly, this new freedom is "a new capacity . . . to be quite free from any fear of the world or life or sin or hell." In short, Barth does not directly refer to any ethical implications at all.

The next circle to look at is the last section of Barth's exposition of "the Royal Man," his reminder that the cross of Jesus forms the final basis and criterium of faith.

Here he does refer to ethics, in a brief reference to the cross of the disciples. As we have already seen, however, he is at pains precisely to distinguish the latter cross from the cross of Jesus himself. His formulation is important:

> The determination of Jesus for death . . . has in the existence of the disciples a counterpart which has an unmistakable likeness for all its inferiority.
>
> [This is] the first thing that is true of those who are His. They would not be His if they did not stand under the law which determined . . . His existence.

Barth then distinguishes between Jesus' cross and the disciples' cross, the primary and secondary *theologia crucis*. He sees a fundamental difference between Jesus' cross (as the symbol for his whole life lived in analogy to God) and the disciples' cross (as the symbol for the lives of the disciples lived in obedience to him). As long as this fundamental difference is kept in mind, it is also necessary to say that without their cross, they do not belong to him at all. His cross is not an example. It has changed their lives fundamentally. His cross has freed them, made them free to accept their own cross as "a welcome sign."

The next circle is found in the section called "the Direction of the Son," which is meant to be the conclusion of paragraph 64 on the exaltation of the Son of Man and therefore the one in which Barth explicitly tries to answer the question: "What is the meaning, or better, the power, of the existence of the one man Jesus Christ . . . for us other men?" This is, of course, the central question of our exploration.

Barth ends this long discussion with a reference to the Trinity and the Holy Spirit, who is mysteriously and miraculously making the transition between Jesus and us (just as the Spirit is eternally making the transition in the partnership of the Father and the Son).

The Spirit makes this transition through *Weisung,* that is, by making us wise in our ways. The Spirit gives direction, which determines the transition from Jesus to us in three forms. First, it is *indication.* It points us to the fixed place of freedom where we must start. We must be what we are in Jesus. An imperative is addressed to us, resting on the indicative of Jesus Christ himself. Second, it is *correction.* The Holy Spirit distinguishes between the possibilities of freedom and "unfreedom." It permits no compromise and allows no cheap grace. Third, it is *instruction.* This brings us to some of Barth's convictions about ethics that have puzzled so many and have been criticized so often. He is convinced that the Lord as the Holy Spirit actually, directly, and concretely instructs us what to do. This is something that ethics, dealing at best with general principles, can, of course, never do. He writes:

> His instruction does not consist merely in the fact that He advances considerations, or provides the material for them. It is certainly part of His instruction to cause or summon us to test ourselves and our situation, to consider most carefully our possibilities and choices. This is the task of theological ethics. . . . But the Spirit is rather more than a professor of theological ethics. He is the One—and this is His instruction—who actually reveals and makes known and imparts and writes on our heart and conscience the will of God as it applies to us concretely here and now, the command of God in the individual and specific form in which we have to respect it in our own situation. The Holy Spirit does, therefore, that concerning which we ourselves, even in the best theological ethics, can only ask. . . . What we are given in [the Spirit's] instruction are not merely principles and general lines of action which leave plenty of room for selection in detailed interpretation—as if it were not the details that really matter! On the contrary, He shows us the only good possibility which there is for us here and now in the freedom of our point of departure.

In this connection he then discusses the nature and importance of the apostolic admonitions of the New Testament. The difficulties for ethical thinking and decision making are obvious.

Because of the Holy Spirit's central role, we need to pay attention to paragraphs 66-68 of *CD* IV/2, the rest of Barth's discussion of "the

Servant as Lord." In all three paragraphs he deals quite extensively with "ethical" issues as well. In paragraph 66, on sanctification, Barth discusses, *inter alia,* "the call to discipleship," "the awakening to conversion," "the praise of works," and "the dignity of the cross." All of these are obviously relevant to "ethical" thinking and behavior. In paragraph 67 he discusses the role of the Spirit in the upbuilding of the Christian community under the basic thesis that the Spirit is the quickening power with which Jesus causes Christianity to grow, sustains it, and orders it, thus fitting it to give a provisional representation of the sanctification of all humanity and human life as it has taken place in him. This again has important ethical overtones. Then, in paragraph 68, he discusses the role of the Spirit in the individual under the basic thesis that the Spirit is the quickening power through which Jesus places a sinful human being in his community and thus gives that human the freedom, in active self-giving to God and fellow human beings as God's witness, to correspond to the love with which God has drawn that person to himself and raised him or her up, overcoming their sloth and misery. Thus this paragraph deals with love. And the idea is that Christian love is a life of free self-giving, in correspondence with God's act of unconditional grace and love in Jesus Christ, and thus a witness to God's own love. The ethical implications become clearer now.

As our next step, we would obviously have to consider the ethics implied in the rest of Barth's doctrine of reconciliation as outlined in Volume IV—the sorely needed missing link! Although all we have of this volume is his draft (published as *The Christian Life*), it is worth serious consideration, especially paragraph 74. Here Barth considers several key concepts under which one might order the ethics of reconciliation (the Christian life, freedom—already used as the key concept in the creation-ethics in *CD* III/4[18]—conversion, repentance, decision, faith, thanksgiving, and especially faithfulness). Finally, he decides on "invocation" or calling on God. He then discusses baptism as an act of calling on God and the beginning of the Christian life, as well as several petitions of the Lord's Prayer. It is well known that he planned to finish with the Lord's Supper. The section on "The struggle for human righteousness," subdivided into "revolt against disorder," "the Lordless powers," "Thy kingdom come" and *"fiat iustitia,"* is relevant for our theme.[19]

Finally, however, one would have to understand this discussion in terms of Barth's general view of the relationship between dogmatics and ethics, which is, of course, notoriously controversial.

On the one hand, critics have repeatedly criticized Barth on the grounds that his theology made ethics utterly impossible, putting to an end all ethical theory and decision making. In a very interesting recent study, R. W. Lovin has reiterated this judgment, saying that Barth's position makes public moral choices impossible.[20]

Of course, this does not mean that Barth has no interest in ethical and even public or political behavior; the contrary is true, as is seen so clearly from his own involvement in ethical and political issues through the years. No, the point is rather that all such actions become arbitrary in his system, because in the final analysis each individual (and in later years each Christian community) must hear and obey the living voice or the concrete command of the living God in a particular situation.

In the very early years of his *crisis*-theology and the commentary on *Romans,* Barth was very harsh in his judgment on ethics and on all human attempts to regulate ethical behavior. The judgment of God meant a crisis for all human attempts to establish themselves, especially ethically! And of course, if everything was under God's judgment, what difference could there really be between good and bad?

Although Barth tried to answer and accommodate early criticism by arguing that ethical thinking and principles could be helpful, to a certain extent, in pointing to the place where the individual (or community) could expect to hear the concrete command, he never really changed his basic conviction that ethical theory cannot give any concrete guidelines or make any specific decisions on behalf of anyone. Only the Holy Spirit can and indeed does—as Barth was confident and sure—precisely that.

One can expect to hear this concrete command in the situation of freedom to which he or she has been called in Jesus Christ. And that situation has certain "contours," certain "signposts," which Barth is trying to reflect on in his dogmatics. One could say that the situation of freedom is the act of God in Jesus Christ: God's unconditional grace and omnipotent mercy active in the person of Jesus Christ. In the process of reflecting on this situation of freedom, the Bible of course plays a very important role.[21] But in the final resort the command is concrete and direct in particular situations, and ethics certainly cannot give us definitive answers.

On the other hand, J. Gustafson, an influential ethicist, speaks for some when he calls Barth's works "the most coherent and comprehensive account of theological ethics in the Protestant tradition." He adds:

> No pages in my personal theological library show as much wear as Karl Barth's *Church Dogmatics,* II/2, chapter 8, entitled "The Command of God" . . . .
>
> Indeed I am convinced that Karl Barth has stated the complete agenda for theological ethics, has made judgments about all the crucial issues, and defended them well from his point of view![22]

Among others who have expressed similar opinions is R. E. Willis, whose *The Ethics of Karl Barth* is undoubtedly the major work on the subject in English literature:

> The *Church Dogmatics* can itself be interpreted as one long, sustained ethical treatise, which focuses throughout on the one overarching action of God in Jesus Christ as the revelation and fulfillment of the ethical, but which also encloses and determines the solution to the problem of correct human action. For Barth, the revelation of God in Jesus Christ is the solution to correct human behaviour. This means that it is both ontologically and paradigmatically prior, and that human action in its widest ramifications and subtlest nuances can only comprise a recognition and acknowledgement and following of the action of God.[23]

Willis, however, has suggested the reason for the critics' ambivalence to Barth's view. In Barth's attempt to answer the criticism that his crisis theology brought an end to all ethics, he emphasized the event of freedom and grace in Jesus Christ as the starting point for all ethical thinking. "No longer total crisis, but total grace becomes the basis of ethical knowledge and behaviour," comments C. C. West. "The foundation of ethics is the divine determination of man in Jesus Christ. . . . Ethics is therefore quite simply 'action in praise of the grace in Jesus Christ.'" Barth now develops "a general ethics of grace,"[24] and the *Church Dogmatics* as a whole, precisely because it is reflecting on the act of God's grace in Jesus Christ, therefore at the same time describes the basis and content of ethics. That is why Willis calls it "ontologically and paradigmatically prior." We can only recognize, acknowledge, and follow that act of grace.

In order to relate this grace-event in Jesus Christ with everyday life, Barth began to use categories like *analogy,*[25] or "parable," "sign," "conformity," "reflection," and so forth. This again gave rise to serious criticism. On the one hand he was criticized because these terms were so vague, not really giving direct ethical guidance in particular situations. At this point Barth then tried to bridge the gap with his appeal to conscience, to the Holy Spirit, to a confessionlike decision making, to a direct and concrete command; in short, to what Honecker calls "decisionism"[26] and Lovin describes as a style of decision making not capable of assisting in the making of public choices. On the other hand, when Barth tried to deduce too many concrete directives from the Christ-event by means of analogies, he was criticized for reading his own social and political positions into the Christ-event. This happened, for example, in the shorter writings *Rechtfertigung und Recht* (1938) and *Christengemeinde und Bürgergemeinde* (1946).

In short, within Barth's view of the relationship between dogmatics and ethics, he would certainly have regarded the miracles (as paradigms of God's grace) as extremely relevant to ethics and human behavior, because we are called to recognize and acknowledge God's style in Jesus Christ. In Jesus we also are made free to follow God's style analogously in our own lives. Barth, however, would have warned that we must not take this as a general principle or slogan to be applied in a casuistic fashion. It is not a new law and not the final answer to the ethical question. Finally, the Holy Spirit must speak the concrete command of God, albeit within the contours, the signposts, of this vision or paradigm in our hearts and minds.

Concluding Remarks

We can therefore conclude that Reformed Protestantism finds in Karl Barth an important witness to testify that the God of Jesus Christ is indeed in a special way the God of the poor.

Of course, Barth is not "canonical." As Bromiley comments, "naive and uncritical acceptance of Barth as a quasi-infallible authority has nothing to commend it." And he adds: "It even runs contrary to Barth's protested adherence to the scripture principle whereby the purity of all theology, his own included, must come under the biblical test."[27]

But it is in our attempt to do this that Barth reminds us not to start thinking from an anthropological perspective, that is, from a particular human need for salvation, thereby limiting the scope of God's salvation in advance. Rather, we are to take Jesus Christ seriously and to start thinking from the perspective of the kingdom, as manifested in Jesus.

It is indeed somewhat ironical that the Reformed tradition has lost sight of this central theme of the gospel, because the Reformed worldview, life-style, and spirituality have always been inclined to accentuate this very point.[28] Whenever we start from the human condition of sin and our need for spiritual reconciliation, or the human condition of misery and our need of physical liberation, we risk making a "social construct of reality" that obscures essential aspects of the gospel of the kingdom, that asks its own favorite questions and provides its own favorite answers.

Barth therefore challenges us to exchange our particularized and often mutually exclusive "paradigms of salvation" for a more inclusive "paradigm of grace in Jesus Christ." Of course, this may solve certain questions, but will also generate new questions. Nevertheless, we shall simply have to address those questions.

Having challenged us, Barth reminds us of the importance of such a vision of God, of the kingdom, of the grace of Jesus Christ for our concrete lives. It is impossible for our day-to-day lives to remain unaffected by such a vision. Admittedly, we cannot change this vision into a general principle or a new human law. We live in freedom and therefore in responsibility. The same vision may inspire each of us to different courses of action, when we analyze the concrete situation and all the factors involved.

Ultimately, all our actions remain under God's judgment, something it is extremely important to keep in mind—especially for Reformed believers, who are so prone to the temptation to exchange Christ's Lordship for our own! Yet this emphasis should not make us passive. The fact that all our actions are sinful does not mean that some actions are not more adequate analogies of God's grace and mercy than others, causing us to seek out and practice those actions in earnest, all the while calling on God. We shall therefore need "an analogical imagination," equipping us for creative thinking and actions in the face of reality itself. And we will need the courage to confess, if necessary.

In short, reading Barth in South Africa today becomes for us an enormous challenge, indeed, a crisis for the church, in particular for the Dutch Reformed Church family.

Karl Barth's "Revolution of God": Quietism or Anarchy?

Charles Villa-Vicencio

A first reading of Barth's *Epistle to the Romans* suggests a carefully hewed middle path that denies legitimacy to both the existing order and revolution. The revolutionary experiences God's command as an injunction to "not doing." Barth's wagging finger is both uncompromising and intriguing: "The revolutionary Titan is far more godless, far more dangerous, than his reactionary counterpart—because he is so much nearer to the truth." Barth insists, however, that "the reactionary [is] also finally in the wrong, despite the wrongness of the revolutionary." Left paralyzed by the realization that tyranny warrants destruction, while the revolutionary in turn needs to have "wrest from his hands the principle of revolution," the Barthian student could be thrust into ethical quietism or despair or both.

Yet being "compelled to 'not doing,' which is turning back to God, [a person] is once again impelled by God to action." This action demands "the demolition of every idol," "the destruction of everything that is." It anticipates "the end of all hierarchies and authorities and intermediaries."[1] This ultimate society is so radically "new" that Barth suggests the need for government will fall away. Nor does he envisage even a dictatorship of the proletariat, thus earning the wrath of those like Lenin who dismissed such "left-wing" idealism as a "childhood disease." The revolution of God, as Barth understood it, is more radical than any human revolution. Lehmann has called it a "permanent revolution," and Marquardt has identified it as the source of "anarchistic" tendencies in Barth.[2]

Quietism or anarchism? It depends on which section of Barth's *Romans* you regard as most important, but also which sections of his subsequent writings you choose to emphasize. Careful attention to both identifies a Barth who "neither theologizes politics nor politicizes theology."[3] But this does not make for a moderate Barth!

The purpose of this essay is to show the pertinence of Barth's theology for revolutionary politics. Had he been writing in an apolitical vacuum, a neutral interpretation of the Barthian corpus could suffice. When he is read ahistorically in the isolation of an academic environment it is possible to ignore the political trauma that gave rise to his theology. But the truth of the matter is that his theology was not written in "quiet times." And today in South Africa only the most insensitive students of theology are allowed the privilege of ivory tower exegesis. What Troeltsch perceived at the turn of the century, we are convinced of: "We theorize and construct in the eye of the storm."[4] At a time when the salvation and damnation of a people is at stake (what theologians call the *Kairos*), all theology inevitably becomes political language.[5] Good theology is, in addition to all else, always iconoclastic in identifying the interest group being served in a particular society. Authentic preaching involves the incessant unmasking of the powers that destroy humanity. The Christian is compelled by the intensity of the times to choose: either to sacralize the existing order—whether by intent or default—or to confront that order by providing implicit or explicit support for the revolution. The balanced see-saw option that avoids touching the ground on either side is simply not possible.

Theology within the Sound of Guns Booming

In his preface to Edwyn Hoskyn's English translation of the *Römerbrief*, Barth reminds his readers that when he wrote the first version of that manuscript in 1918 "it required only a little imagination . . . to hear the sound of the guns booming away in the north."[6] Yet to subordinate Barth's theology to his politics would be a form of reductionism. He dismissed natural theology as the "arch enemy of all true theology,"[7] and his chief passion was to understand the nature of the God who revealed himself only in Christ, and whom Barth confronted in "the strange new world" of the Bible.[8] Yet toward the end of his life he would state quite emphatically that his theology, grounded as it was in the Bible, "was never a private affair." "Its theme is God for the world, God for man, heaven for earth. This means that my theology always had a strong political side, explicit and implicit."[9] "I decided for theology," he stated, "because I felt the need to find a better basis for my social action."[10] Although Marquardt's controversial thesis *Theologie und Sozialismus* comes close to reducing Barth's theology to his socialist commitment, it does show a lasting socialist commitment that both forms and is formed by Barth's theology. Similarly, Eberhard Busch, in his biography of Barth, has convincingly demonstrated the relationship between Barth's more general political praxis and his theology.[11]

The contours of Barth's political engagement define the continuity and discontinuity of different phases of his theology. Throughout his life Barth expressed his theology at the nexus points of history. Thurneysen speaks of the "inward affliction of a pastor tormented by the conflict between the traditional theology of his time and on the other hand the grim reality of the world."[12] Marquardt refers to Barth turning to theology to seek "the organic connection between the Bible and the newspaper, the new world and the collapsing bourgeois order."[13] The "red pastor of Safenwil" identified the gross inadequacy of existing theological resources to deal with the socioeconomic and political dimensions of his ministry. Here he discovered the contextual significance of the Bible. Here too his *Krisis* theology was born. It was written between the worldview of traditional theology and the world of the Bible, between the values of the Bible and the contradictions of an alienated social order.

The Quest for a Theological Basis for Social Action

During the early period of his writing, Barth understood the transcendence of God to mean the contradiction of all that exists. God could only with difficulty be accommodated within the existing order, his purpose being "to overthrow and set right."[14] Many of Barth's formulations were quite undialectical: "Jesus *is* the movement for social justice, and the movement for social justice *is* Jesus in the present."[15] Echoing standard Marxian critique, he rejected the church's understanding of the relationship between "spirit and matter, inner and outer, heaven and earth." Confronted by social misery, the church had taken refuge in the Spirit, in the inner life and in heaven. "The church had preached, instructed and consoled, but she has *not helped*."[16] In making this critique he rejected capitalism as among the greatest "atrocities of life" and private property as sin, "because property is self-seeking," that which "stands in the way of the coming of God's kingdom to earth." Christians, he argued, are bound not merely to "*say* that the material situation of the proletariat must become a different and a better one": a follower of Jesus "seizes and employs a means to lead this goal to realization." Barth's concern is for a program of action, arguing that "real socialism is real Christianity in our time."[17]

Barth's apparent disappointment with the material failure of the socialist cause led to his radically revised Christology; this, in turn, became the basis for his understanding of the revolution of God.[18] The 1918 Russian revolution failed to realize what many socialists had expected, and Barth's faith in revolutionary praxis was shattered. His 1919 Tambach lecture marks his parting from the religious socialists. In this lecture Barth radically distanced God's kingdom from the revolutions of people, but even at this point he continued to regard human protest as "an integral moment in the Kingdom of God."[19] In the wake of Tambach came the second edition of *Romans*, published in 1921. Its purpose was "the censure of the red brother."[20] In *Romans*, Barth writes that God's unqualified No is spoken against all human revolution, yet not as a negation of revolution *per se*. Rather, it is the basis for a more radical revolution—God's revolution. Despite Barth's uncompromising rejection of the Promethean human revolutionary effort as being wrong before God, even if justified before the bar of history, he continued to hold to the conviction that the gospel "displays a certain inclination to side with those who are . . . ready for revolution."[21] God's No did not entail moral or political paralysis for Barth. In 1922 (the same year in which the third edition of *Romans* was written) Barth argued that God's No is really Yes:

> *This* judgment is grace. *This* condemnation is forgiveness. *This* death is life. *This* hell is heaven. *This* fearful God is a loving father who takes the prodigal in his arms. The crucified is the one raised from the dead. And the explanation of the cross as such is eternal life.

He then continues, "God is the Yes in its fullness: it is only in order that we may *understand* him as God that we must pass through his No."[22] This Yes to the world appears even stronger in the Tambach lecture, where Barth emphasises the need for an affirmation of this world and the need "to enter into the God-given restlessness and into critical opposition to life." This, for him, was a means for restoring God's creation, which he defines as "the revolution which is before all revolutions."[23] God's permanent revolution transcends all human revolutions precisely because it is the eschatological restoration of God's original revolution. From the perspective of the rulers of this world this is tantamount to anarchy.

Yet many students of Barth argue that it was during this period that Barth turned away from an overt form of political theology. Jüngel suggests such a change came even earlier, with "The Christian

Faith and History," written in 1910.[24] Here Barth argued that it is only through faith, and not through historical investigation, that divine revelation can be known. "The Christ external to us is the Christ within us."[25] Some have perceived this redirection as a shift away from a concern with historical and material manifestations of God's presence to a personal and inward experience of it.[26] While this emphasis, which is stronger in some publications than others from 1910 onward, cannot be ignored, neither should it be isolated from other emphases in Barth's theology. The experience of faith, however abstract, is necessarily related to concrete reality. "Experience, praxis, or whatever one wants to call it, is the obvious presupposition, the source of all religious utterances."[27] In other words, whatever the nature of the experience of faith, its origin was to be found in historical events. This relationship between faith and history, however hesitantly he formulated it during this period, became the basis for what is commonly called Barth's dialectical period.

These years—essentially from the publication of the second edition of *Romans* in 1921 to *Anselm: Fides Quaerens Intellectum* in 1928—were experienced by Barth as years lived "between the times" *(Zwischen den Zeiten)*. During this period, Barth focused his theology on the infinite qualitative difference between God and humankind. If earlier he had emphasized human effort, he now focused decisively on God. Immanence had given way to a transcendence so radical that to affirm the incarnation was scarcely possible.[28] This phase prepared the way for two important radical dimensions of Barth's later theology. In rejecting Feuerbach's reduction of theology to anthropology and in separating God from humankind, Barth affirmed a God greater than the best idea of God humankind could either project or approximate.[29] Already in the second edition of *Romans* he had argued,

> Grace means divine impatience, discontent, dissatisfaction: it means that the whole is required. Grace is the enemy of everything, even of the most indispensable "interim ethic." Grace is the axe laid at the root of the good conscience which the politician and the civil servant always wish to enjoy. . . .[30]

This sense of "divine impatience" became the linchpin of Barth's mature understanding of the revolution of God. Contrary to what many commentators allow, this "quiet" period of Barth's theological quest provided a firm foundation for his most revolutionary politics. Apparently, he was well aware of this, continuing to relate his quest for a transcendent God to his interest in political ethics. This is nowhere clearer than in his essay on Feuerbach, to which we have already referred: "The church," he tells us, "will be free of Feuerbach's question only when its ethics have been radically separated from both the ancient and modern hypotheses. The church will again win belief that its God is no illusion—but never until then."[31]

Barth had in these terms found the "basis for [his] social action." He rejected the reduction of theology to politics in the form of liberal immanentism. He also refused to legitimate any particular political ideology by affirming an otherworldly form of transcendence that would leave the realm of human action untouched by the judgment of God. For Barth the authentic meeting ground between God's transcendence and human politics was to be found in the concept of analogy. In his development of the concept of *analogia fidei*, suggests Paul Lehmann, Barth "was pioneering a metaphorical interpretation of the knowledge and obedience of faith."[32] Reminding us of Barth's challenge *"Lassen die Kritiker noch kritischer werden"* (let the critics become more critical) in the preface to the second edition of *Romans*, Lehmann points to the historical and political nature of Barth's most traditional and orthodox language. Barth attempted "to liberate orthodoxy from orthodox literalism." Says Lehmann,

> As a young tutor in theology in the Seminary, I learned through being on the losing end of more than one fierce theological debate [with Barth] how intense and magisterial this repudiation of dialectical dogmatics could be. . . . He himself seems not to have been fully cognizant of this creative frontier of his thought.

Barth's quest was for the "essential metaphor"—that which identifies what is holy in the most concrete dimensions of history. He had anticipated what Horkheimer would call the "theological moment" in politics, without which "no matter how skilful, [politics] in the last analysis is mere business."[33] Without this "moment" or "metaphor," the possibility of breaking the stalemate of power politics is minimal, and hope of creating something radically new is lost. Lehmann's perception of the Barthian metaphor demands that even his seemingly most ahistorical, ethereal, and pietistic language be looked at yet again in the light of the political context within which it was written.

If this analysis is correct, Barth's reference to analogy in his 1919 Tambach lecture also needs to be given heavier emphasis than most commentators allow. It not only signals greater continuity in the Barthian corpus than is often realized, but it also identifies the political significance of a great deal of his less obviously political concerns during the so-called quiet period.[34] Barth's understanding of analogy came to form the basis of his mature theology and the dynamic of his theology of the revolution of God. His understanding of the state as analogous to the kingdom of God required that the state be evaluated in the light of God's intended purpose for creation—and this requirement constituted the revolutionary thrust of Barth's church-state doctrine.

Barth had firmly established his theological framework by the time Hitler came to power in 1933. This altered political situation compelled him to speak out against the state.[35] On the basis of his understanding of the sovereignty of God, radically different from but always in relation to history, he held theology and politics in creative tension. Barth addressed the Jewish question with a resolve that many others failed to show.[36] Yet, as the leading architect of the Barmen Declaration, he must share the blame leveled against its signatories for failing to address anti-Semitism explicitly. Barth, in fact, accepted the criticism against him and the Confessing Church for being silent on this matter.[37] Barmen did, nevertheless, provide a theoretical framework for political resistance. For Barth this was a *first step,* however inadequately developed in relation to such specific political issues. Indeed, Barth would write: "It was on the truth of the sentence that God is One that the Third Reich of Adolf Hitler made shipwreck."[38] In the postwar years it was this same dynamic that caused him to keep silent when the Soviet Union invaded Hungary in 1956. He insisted that it was not the task of theology to legitimate a state that declared its moral superiority over that of an enemy state. Rather, theology's task was to deabsolutize a political system that justifies itself by anti-communist fanaticism. "I regard anti-communism," he said, "as a matter of principle to be an evil even greater than communism."[39] The West's ideological No to communism is cancelled by God's No to Western perceptions of its own values as those of the angel of light. In so doing the divine No becomes the basis for a Yes to what is radically new in world politics, transcending both Marxist-Leninist forms of socialism and Western capitalism.

Politics: Bourgeois and Anarchistic

The divine No, so intimately related to God's Yes, means that God's revolution is the limit imposed on all human revolutions as well as the source and inspiration of the ideal of a successful and permanent revolution. The "pathos" of God's revolution is for Barth just that. The revolutionary "stands so strangely near to God" precisely because of his or her total rejection of the existing order. Yet, determined to destroy the romantic idealism surrounding revolution, Barth argues that even the revolutionary who "aims at the Revolution by which the true Order is to be inaugurated" is invariably trapped in "discontent and hatred and insubordination, of rebellion and demolition." Ultimately, this is not revolution; it is reactionism. For Barth the revolution of God is the corrective to all revolutions. Participation in God's revolution involves "the great opportunity of willing to do what God does"—it involves loving one's neighbor.[40] This revolution, suggests Paul Lehmann, enables the human revolutionary "to be and to stay human in the world" and, in so doing, prevents the revolution "from devouring its own children."[41]

Since we in South Africa read Barth "in the eye of the storm," one can interpret this caution as counterrevolutionary, and some liberation theologians have criticized Barth's theology for failing to deliver the necessary liberating thrust in a concrete situation of oppression. James Cone's observation in this regard is representative of many of Barth's critics who take him up on this point. Suggesting that "Jesus the liberator is not central in Barth's Christology," and that "to be outside of this community [of the poor and oppressed] is to be in a place where one is excluded from the possibility of hearing and obeying God's Word of liberation," he argues that Barth fails to "hear the cries and the moans of the people." [42] In addressing himself to this apparent dissension between Barth and liberation theologians, Hunsinger concludes: "I think Barth is right in principle whereas the liberationists are right in practice." Conceding that Barth has "something important to learn from them," he also identifies what Míguez-Bonino refers to as a "dangerous tendency" in liberation theology to collapse love for God into love of neighbor, which could result in "deifying history or humanity itself." We can resist this temptation, suggests Hunsinger, only "by something like Barth's unqualified precedence for God's Word."[43] Gollwitzer seems to have identified the essential nature of Barth's post-Safenwil dilemma in arguing that social "classes hold us all tenaciously fast," and that Barth's bourgeois academic milieu ultimately rendered a "bourgeois slant even to a theology anti-bourgeois in tendency."[44]

Yet when Barth's work is read in a crisis situation—within "the sound of guns booming" in Crossroads or Soweto—the revolutionary tendency of his words can be rediscovered and his theology appropriated by that section of the church which is part of the liberation of South Africa. In this situation four specific dimensions of Barth's theology take on special significance.

To love one's neighbor. The pertinent political question that arises in Barth's theology of the revolution of God has to do with what it means to love one's neighbor in a specific situation. Barth is quite clear on this point. It means that "we cannot wish to uphold the present order."[45] To love one's neighbor means to move "individual egoism" to "collective egoism" in political and economic structures that are national and global. In this context Barth addresses the cultural and economic exploitation of Asia and Africa by the First World, as well as questions of economic socialism. In so doing he raises questions about the function of private property in society, the division of labor, and the use of modern technology.[46] Barth's concern to understand the economic implications of love resulted in a lifelong commitment to a form of social democracy that left him critical of both East and West:

> The injustice of using one man by another merely as a means to his own ends, as a mere instrument, once rested on a foundation of private capital, and still does in the West. Yet it is by no means impossible . . . that this injustice can perpetuate itself in a different form on a different basis, namely, on that of state socialism which is in fact directed by a ruling and benefit-deriving group.[47]

Barth asks a vital question: "Why does the exercise of Christian love so seldom make any significant impression on the world . . . ?"[48] This question, when asked of the church located in situations of revolution, has revolutionary intent. However, for Barth, there remains a more fundamental issue, one that deals with what he called the "Archimedean point" from which society is enabled to change direction and share in God's revolution.

Justification by faith. Barth locates this "point" in his rediscovery of the inherent link between justification and social justice.[49] He introduces an important political dimension to the "escapist" center of that kind of pietistic religiosity which resides in most proletarian communities. This is, to use Barth's own words, "the *Archimedean point* from which the soul and, with the soul, society are moved."[50] To a revolutionary struggle in a religious community, this spiritual center can be more dangerous than the most revolutionary Marxist theory. When an oppressed people realize that God does not will their oppression and that their political and economic liberation is an inherent part of their God-given gift of salvation, they become an irrepressible constituency of people no oppressor can afford to ignore. The Kairos Document affirms this link between the spiritual and political quite explicitly, and the South African regime has responded quite characteristically in seeking to undermine this kind of theological protest.

Choosing the side of the poor. South Africa bolsters its ideology

53

of oppression of the poor with a fierce "anti-Marxist" cry—the kind so roundly condemned by Barth. Yet precisely because so many people are brainwashed by the government-controlled media into believing that the "political dimension" of Latin American theology must be ascribed to the influence of Marxist atheism, it is important to show that other theological traditions also teach Christians to oppose all forms of political and economic exploitation. Barth's Word of God provides this kind of alternative, not as a basis for conceding the media's attack on liberation theology but rather as a means for verifying the latter's conclusions via another route.

Affirming a traditional Protestant theological position, Barth could say with the conviction of any liberation theologian: "God stands at every time unconditionally and passionately on this side and only on this side: always against the exalted and for the lowly, always against those who have rights and for those from whom they are robbed and taken away."[51] The poor in South Africa carry with them a sense of missionary-imposed Protestant piety, and those who minister to them find in Barth's theology a tradition in relation to which they can articulate their quest for liberation. The immediate theological need of the poor in this country is for a theology that pronounces a radical No to the structures of oppression legitimated by a heretical Christian ideology. Barth provides precisely this.

Theological "anarchy." Barth's affirmation of God's No to all human effort, whether in support of the reactionary status quo or of a revolutionary dictatorship, raises questions about his alleged anarchistic tendency. His theology leaves no doubt that God's Yes is ultimately uttered against the reactionary "despite the wrongness of the revolutionary."[52] Tillich recognized a "destructive" dimension in Barth's theology when he warned that "an instrument that is a mighty weapon in warfare may be an inconvenient tool for use in the building trade."[53] Hunsinger, in turn, concludes that Barth "argues with the radicality of the anarchists."[54] And, when one reads Barth's address in Basel on the bicentennial anniversary of Mozart's birth celebrated in 1956, one cannot but discern a certain reckless abandon in his speech. When this "recklessness" transcends his music appreciation and penetrates his politics, one realizes that Barth was no more a cautious and balanced political theologian than Mozart was a musician of equilibrium.

> Mozart's center is not like that of the great theologian Schleiermacher, identical with balance, neutralization and finally indifference. What happened in this center is rather a splendid annulment of balance, a

turn in the strength of which the light rises and the shadow winks but does not disappear; happiness outdistances sorrow without extinguishing it and the "Yes" rings stronger than the existing "No." Notice the *reversal* of the great dark and the little bright experiences in Mozart's life! "The rays of the sun disperse the night"—that's what you hear at the end of the *Magic Flute*. The play may or must still proceed or start from the very beginning. But it is a play which in some Height or Depth is winning or has already won. This directs and characterizes it. One will never perceive equilibrium, and for that reason uncertainty or doubt, in Mozart's music.[55]

Anarchism is often used as a synonym for *chaos*. This is not, however, how it would be used in classical debate, and it would certainly be wrong to suggest that Barth favored sociopolitical chaos. According to a fairly standard definition of the term, *anarchism* is "the organisation of society on the basis of voluntary cooperation, and especially without the agency of political institutions, i.e. the state."[56] Anarchists tend to regard the state as an instrument of the ruling class used to dominate and exploit the people. Certainly Barth had an abiding suspicion of unfettered political power and saw the revolution of God as a corrective to the human abuse of power. Yet he also had a high regard for the state—arguing that "if the state has perverted its God-given authority, it cannot be honoured better than by this [the church's] criticism." Indeed, "Jesus would, in actual fact, have been an enemy of the state if he had not dared, quite calmly, to call King Herod a 'fox.'"[57]

Although Barth deabsolutized the existing order and criticized the revolution from the left, showing an anarchistic tendency, he believed that the state would be unnecessary only eschatologically. The dimension of anarchy one discerns in his thought is *theological* anarchy. Unlike political anarchists he did not believe that political institutions were necessarily instruments of the abuse of power. For him the state was ordained to be an instrument of God, and provided that the state remained in subjection to God it could be a means for furthering the creative and liberating purpose of creation. "It is *only* in relation to God that the evil of the existing order is really evil." "*Our* 'new' is not the 'new.'"[58]

For Barth, a just socioeconomic and political order was simply not possible in an unredeemed society where, however egalitarian its intent, egotism and greed are merely veiled under such ideologies as economic competition while being legitimated and sanctioned by prevailing laws and doctrines. Barth's concern was that in this unredeemed society the fundamental problems of inhumanity and exploitation were not addressed.[59] The history of world revolutions showed that these problems were not resolved in postrevolutionary societies. His ultimate hope for a "successful" revolution would therefore have to be located elsewhere. It is not *grounded* in a new political order, but in the possibility of a "new person" and "new creation," which would include a new political order. For Barth this is necessarily a consequence of an "integral moment" in which God's "original revolution"—God's creation as originally given—breaks into history.[60]

Anarchism or quietism? Is the Christian morally paralyzed as he or she awaits the eschatological moment when God will do what is humanly impossible? Alternatively, are Christians to be so caught up in God's No to all human political options that they can be seen only as anarchists? Barth's answer is decisive: "A protest against a particular social order, to be sure, is an integral moment in the Kingdom of God, and there have been dark, blundering godless times when this moment of protest was suppressed and hidden."[61] Similarly, his concept of analogy, which always upholds a separation between God and the world, allows for an analogical and parabolic relationship between human endeavor and the kingdom of God. The state, he insisted, is a parable of the kingdom of God, required to structure itself in relation to the demands of the kingdom.[62] The church, in turn, is required to be a "reminder of the justice of the Kingdom of God . . . and a promise of its future manifestation. . . . She can and should show them that there already exists on earth an order based on that great transformation of the human situation and directed towards its manifestation."[63]

Barth's hope extends well beyond what any immediate human revolution can produce, but for him, "when the great hope is present, *small* hopes must always arise for the immediate future."[64] This use of God's revolution, which at first sight seems to negate all human responsibility, makes Barth's theology an inspirational source for sustained human participation in a continuing quest for something more than any particular society can deliver. In this context his deabsolutizing of the revolution and his relativizing of impetuous activism are shaped by his commitment to ensure that all political action remains human in what is all too often a dehumanizing struggle. This reflective moment may indeed distract from the spontaneous will to action. But in his theology Barth makes a profound theological contribution to the Marxist distinction between thoughtless *practice* and critical *praxis*. For Marx, the latter necessarily includes critical analysis and reflection as a basis for and a consequence of action.[65] Barth both radicalizes and deabsolutizes Marx's revolutionary theory.[66]

A Christological Basis

Marquardt correctly observes that "for Barth, 'God's revolution' was no mere stopgap for the failures of the bolshevist revolution as it ossified into an establishment."[67] Rather, Barth's understanding of the revolution of God is a direct consequence of his doctrine of God and more particularly of his Christology. His entire theological quest was an attempt to articulate, in a responsible manner, the nature of the relationship between eternity and time, between God and humanity, between theology and anthropology. From the point of view of theological ethics, his quest was for a theological basis for social action.

The early Barth found the link between the revolution of God and social action in the person of Jesus. The later Barth redefined this link in relation to the two natures of Christ,[68] the *distinction* between which natures[69] has political significance. We can observe this distinction between the divine and human natures of Christ in God's No to human revolution. The *unity* of the two natures[70] is, in turn, not only christologically imperative but also politically important. Barth expresses passionately and urgently this unifying transcendence of what is infinitely different:

> We may believe that God can and must only be absolute in contrast to all that is relative, exalted in contrast to all that is lowly, active in contrast to all suffering, . . . transcendent in contrast to all immanence, in short that He can and must be only the "Wholly Other." But such beliefs are shown to be quite untenable and corrupt and pagan, by the fact that God does in fact be and do this in Jesus Christ.[71]

This relationship between the two natures of Christ becomes the basis of Barth's concept of the revolution of God as we have discussed it here. The inner material connection between God and humanity, between time and eternity, between God's revolution and human revolutions is located not merely in an *analogia entis* but an *analogia relationis*.[72] To understand this concept of an analogical *relationship* between God and humanity—a God who is always more than humanity but always related to humanity not only in being but also in praxis—is to understand the relevance of the revolution of God for human political action.

A Crisis Reading of Barth

Barth, like most formative theologians, is claimed by readers of different ideological persuasions. A literary text does not mean simply what is read within it, but takes on a life of its own. It becomes independent of its author. Yet to do justice to the text the reader must enquire about the context from which it emerged and weigh the differing, latent, and often contradictory emphases within it.

It requires a crisis situation such as that which prevails in South Africa today to discern the antiestablishment bias of Barth's thought, which is so often, on balance, outweighed by traditional theological concerns. Barth was of a different age and was not obliged to face all the programmatic demands the church is obliged to face in South Africa today. However, he did recognize with a clarity denied many of his peers that "we do not really know Jesus if we do not know him as this poor man, as this partisan of the poor and finally as this revolutionary."[73] This dimension of Barth's theology makes James Cone, in spite of his criticism of Barth, argue against those "Barthians who used him to justify doing nothing about the struggle for justice," and to state, "I have always thought that Barth was closer to me than to them."[74]

Theology and Socialism

Robin Petersen

In recent years the relationship between theology and socialism has once again become a crucial issue on the theological agenda. Both at a practical level, where Christians are engaged in the human struggle for personal, political, and economic liberation, and at a theoretical level, where theologians are reflecting upon this liberating praxis, the issue has become a "theological crux."[1]

Within the South African context, it is increasingly acknowledged that the struggle against apartheid is also fundamentally a struggle against capitalism. This "paradigm shift" from race to class analysis has, in many instances, left theology behind. What was before theologically and ethically incontrovertible—one's opposition to racial discrimination—has become far more complex and, in certain quarters, ambiguous. Here one parts company with many well-intentioned fellow travelers, and here one finds new and somewhat strange "comrades" in the struggle. Here the hoary beast of "anticommunism" raises its head and here also the theological reflections on our "common praxis" for a socialist society become far more complicated.

In this demanding situation our historical resources as theologians are limited. As a Reformed theologian committed to the struggle for a nonracial, democratic, and socialist future for this country and deeply challenged by the insights and commitments of liberation theology, I discovered through the provocative work of F.-W. Marquardt and George Hunsinger's collection of essays[2] the lasting socialist commitment of the seminal Reformed theologian of the twentieth century, Karl Barth. In fact, as Marquardt has argued, not only was Barth a socialist, but his theology arose from within his socialist praxis, as a means of both giving ground to and explicating it.

Returning to Barth's theology with this new insight as a kind of heuristic tool, I rediscovered for myself the relevance and helpfulness of Barth in responding to the theological and political imperative of socialism from within a Reformed context. What follows here is an attempt to draw the contours of this sadly neglected *socialist* Barth, focusing on three areas: a brief biography of the socialist Barth; an analysis of his statements on socialism, communism, and capitalism, including a look at how he integrated certain crucial Marxian insights into his theology; and, finally and most importantly, an analysis of the theological basis and grounding of his socialism.[3]

A Biography of Socialist Praxis

Barth's early socialist commitment and praxis are fairly well known, although usually discounted by those for whom the later Barth is a paragon of pragmatic "reasonableness," standing very wisely "between East and West." The upshot of this disregard is twofold: first, the real extent and depth of his early socialist praxis are neither disclosed nor taken seriously, and second, the fundamental socialist continuity between the early praxis and theology and the mature theory of *Church Dogmatics* is ignored. This in turn has enabled the theology of the *Dogmatics* to be led captive into a politically conservative or liberal exile, a truly "strange land" for a man whose theology has aptly been described as one of "permanent revolution."[4]

The research by Marquardt, Gollwitzer, and Hunsinger[5] on Barth's socialist praxis need not be repeated here. They have decisively shown that his socialist commitment remained unflagging to the end of his life, that the fiery passion of Safenwil might have dimmed but was never extinguished, and that his theology cannot be separated from his socialism. On this last point, Hunsinger's perceptive insight into the political context of the major developments of Barth's theology is particularly helpful.[6] There is no doubt that his theology was decisively influenced by his commitment to socialist praxis and his wish to ground this in a substantial and solid theological foundation. Barth himself confirmed this view in an interview given in 1956: "I decided for theology because I felt a need to find a better basis for my social action."[7]

Socialism, Marxism, Communism, and Capitalism

In the last few years of his life, when asked the question, "Were you a Marxist?" Barth responded emphatically: "No, I never was that, decidedly not. I was never a doctrinaire Socialist."[8] In the first edition of *Romans,* however, Barth looked forward with hope to the day when "the now-dying ember of Marxist dogma will blaze forth anew as the world truth, when the socialist church will be raised from the dead in a world become socialist."[9] How can we reconcile these two statements? Had Barth himself forgotten how radical he had once sounded, or is there still a basic continuity and coherence between these points of view? In this chapter I will address these issues through an analysis of Barth's writings on the subjects of socialism, capitalism, Marxism, and communism, and will advance the following five theses:

1. Barth was consistently critical of, and opposed to, the capitalist economic order.

2. While from his earliest years he rejected Marxism as a "world view," he accepted and integrated many aspects of the Marxian theoretical analysis into his thinking.

3. His lifelong commitment to socialism was fundamentally "practical."

4. He had a critical but basically open attitude toward "actually existing communism."

5. His later position "between East and West" was neither a theological abstraction nor a weak neutrality, but was grounded in his hope for a truly socialist future in both East and West.

Capitalism: A Revolutionary Critique

In one of Barth's earliest published articles, "Jesus Christ and the movement for social justice" (1911), and more particularly in his open letter responding to the Safenwil industrialist Hussy, who had vehemently attacked the article, it is very apparent that the young Barth both understood and endorsed the radical Marxian critique of the capitalist order.[10] Capitalism, he states, "is the system of production which makes the proletariat into a dependent wage earner whose existence is constantly insecure." Exploitation of the worker is possible because the means of production are the *private property* of one of the co-workers, namely, the boss, the factory owner." By this ownership, the profits of the enterprise are also accounted for as the "factory owner's *private property*," and the workers who have contributed their labor to the process are paid merely a pitiful wage. Such a system is ethically unjust, in that the one "becomes a distinguished person, amasses capital, lives in a beautiful house, and is granted all the pleasures of life, while the other must live from hand to mouth." This creates a fundamental "class contradiction"—"the daily crime of capitalism." The whole system, argues Barth, "especially its underlying principle—private property—must fall."[11]

It is clear from this article that Barth's rejection of capitalism in his early years was fundamental and structural and not merely an expression of moral indignation against some of the excesses of early *laissez-faire* capitalism. This understanding is extremely significant as it locates Barth clearly within a "revolutionary socialist"—as opposed to a "reformist liberal"—position. For Barth it was not enough merely to ameliorate some of the rough edges of capitalism; what was required was the overthrow of its base—private ownership of the means of production.

When Barth's later writings are analyzed, it becomes apparent that this radical and structural critique of capitalism remains with him to the end. His section on "Work" in *CD* III/4 reveals this continuity in particular. First, he rejects capitalism because of the competitive nature of work it embodies: "work under the sign of competition will always imply, as such, work in the form of conflict and will always be an inhuman activity, and therefore an activity which, in spite of every conceivable alleviation or attempt at relief can never stand before the command of God" (p. 451).

Second, given the private ownership of the means of production, "the modern industrial process" in the West rests in "the principle of exploitation of some by others," enabling the capitalists to "earn more than they are entitled to" (p. 542). This occurs in spite of the power of the organized working class and the contract between unions and employees, which has done much to better the material conditions of the working class and to "balance" the interests of the two classes. Barth's indictment of this "balanced" feature of the modern industrial state is striking: "This is social injustice in a form which is less blatant than simple competition . . . but which is even more oppressive and provoking in its ostensible show of justice" (p. 542).

Clearly there is a fundamental continuity in Barth's analysis of capitalism. Because of the basic socialist and Marxian content of the critique, Barth can never fully endorse liberal efforts to reform the system. His *theoretical* critique is revolutionary to the end: the system needs to be overthrown, not just to have its excesses curbed. No amount of social tinkering or compensatory or ameliorative measures can alter its fundamental injustice, against which the command of God is directed.

If we see that Barth's attitude toward capitalism is the same in both his earlier, "more-radical" stage and his more pragmatic, mature stage, it becomes clear that Barth remains fundamentally and decisively committed to the "revolutionary" overcoming of the capitalist order. What changes is the basis and locus of this revolution; it shifts from his earlier vision of the revolutionary potential of the international socialist movement in the period up to 1918 to his hopes for the Christian community and the "great positive possibility" of love that becomes the "essentially revolutionary action."[12]

Marxism as a Worldview

Barth's use of the pejorative term *doctrinaire socialist* to describe what he means by the term *Marxist* is instructive, as it reveals his basic antipathy to the overall theoretical scheme of Marxism. From his earliest writings Barth sees Marxism as a "world view" as being incompatible with Christianity. Marxism is in fact a pseudo-religion: it cannot dispense with the development of a "basic, declarative ideology and mythology, i.e., some sort of overworld has to be dreamed into it too," which brings about "the founding of a new religion" (*CD* I/2, 323).

His rejection of the ideological structure of Marxism meshes with Barth's rejection of all alliances between Christianity and any secular worldview. But significantly, rejection of a system does not mean rejection of its individual components. Concerning all worldviews, Barth writes:

> Faith is radically dialogical to them. In the last respect it has never taken them seriously, even though it has fiercely opposed them or intimately allied itself to them. It accepts no responsibility for their foundation, structure, validity or propagation. It moves within their territory but cannot be detained at their frontiers. (*CD* III/2, 9)

We are concerned with this "moving within the territory," as it is here that Barth integrates certain crucial Marxian insights into his thinking. Barth's critique of capitalism and his theology of work are central to this integration. Equally important and revealing clear Marxian undertones are the relationship Barth posits between theory and praxis, his radical critique of religion, and his theology of revolution.

Theory and Praxis

Marx's philosophy of praxis is well known, best summarized in his famous eleventh thesis on Feuerbach. Barth, within his own theological center, clearly affirmed this priority of praxis. Theory and praxis are inseparable for Barth, and the dogmatic task is a directly ethical one. The preface to the first volume of *Church Dogmatics*, written during the German church struggle of the 1930s, spells this out: "I am firmly convinced that we cannot reach the clarifications, especially in the broad field of politics, which are necessary today and to which theology today might have a word to say . . . without having previously reached those comprehensive clarifications in theology and about theology itself, with which we should be concerned here" (*CD* I/1, xiii). Barth grounds this theory-praxis dialectic in two areas, his doctrine of God and his anthropology, coordinated and centered in his Christology.

For Barth, God can never simply be "a reality . . . which does not affect or claim men or awaken them to responsibility or redeem them, i.e., a theoretical reality" (*CD* II/1, 163). God is always and only known in God's act, and that act is the revolutionary transformation of all that is. God, writes Barth, is "the fact which not only illuminates but materially transforms all things and everything in all things" (*CD* II/1, 258). The obvious similarities between this statement and Marx's eleventh thesis have been perceptively noted by Marquardt.[13]

Barth's central definition of God reveals again this concern to hold together act and being, theory and praxis. "God is He who lives and loves in freedom" (*CD* II/1, 257ff.). Interesting too is Marquardt's insight in tracing the aetiology of this primary definition of God to an early description by Barth of truly ethical, socialist praxis.[14]

Turning to Barth's anthropology, we see the same theory-praxis dialectic. "Only the doer of the Word is the real hearer, for it is the Word of the Living God addressed to the living man absorbed in the work and action of life" (*CD* I/2, 742). For Barth, "theory and practice cannot be separated in the human world" (*CD* II/1, 661). The coordination and center of these two grounds are found in the living, acting person, Jesus Christ. From this center human action as a parable of God's action can be effectively secured as liberating praxis.

Religion

In theological circles, Barth's attack on religion is as well known as Marx's. "The world that professes to be religious is actually the world in its worst form."[15] The theological contours of this rejection are also clear and well known. Religion is a "criminal arrogance"; it is the ultimate human presumption in its grasping after God through piety, worship, and morality. Humankind's search for God is in fact its resistance to God, and it is here, at the religious center, that human rebellion is the greatest. Without gainsaying the theological basis of this critique, it is equally possible to trace the impetus for this development in other directions as well: the direction of Barth's socialist praxis and his understanding of Marx and Feuerbach at this crucial point.

Barth's reading of Marx and Feuerbach had exposed him to their materialist critique of religion. The actions of ninety-three German professors in support of the Kaiser's war effort had convinced an already suspicious Barth of both the class basis of liberal theology and its vulnerability to the critique of Feuerbach and Marx.[16] Both in theory and praxis, the liberal theological model confirmed, rather than overcame, this critique. Barth's disillusionment with the basically liberal categories of religious socialism radicalized his position, and he was thus forced to affirm Feuerbach while simultaneously attempting to overcome him. This radicalized his theology, resulting in his construction of the God-faith axis as the *Aufhebung* of religion. To rescue the truth of God from its captivity to ideological suspicion, it is necessary, argues Barth, to make certain that "man's relation with God is in every respect, in principle, an irreversible relation."[17]

Yet not only the truth but the *reality* and *relevance* of God need to be rescued from this critique. This Barth achieved in three ways: first, by a socially reflected concept of God, where God can be spoken of only "when the concern is with the reality of man";[18] second, in his christological center and in his recovery of the "two natures" doctrine, according to which God and human beings are held together in inseparable unity; and third, in his response to Feuerbach in terms of orthopraxis: "The church will be free of Feuerbach's [and Marx's] question only when its ethics have been radically separated from both the ancient and modern hypostases. Then the church will again win belief that God is no illusion—but never until then."[19]

Exoteric, Not Esoteric

Exoteric, not esoteric, is how Barth defined his socialism in contrast with Tillich's. As he was never committed to socialism as a theory, he was never "detained at the frontiers" of theoretical disputes and debates within socialism. In a letter to Tillich in 1933 he stated: "Membership in the SPD does not mean for me a confession to the idea and world view of socialism. . . . Membership in the SPD means for me simply a practical political decision."[20]

As we have seen, Barth always regarded capitalism even in its most liberal and progressive form to be against the command of God. But he was never dogmatic about the alternative. As he stated in "The Christian Community and the Civil Community," the church, "in choosing between the various socialist possibilities (social-liberalism? co-operativism? syndicalism? free-trade? moderate or radical Marxism?) will always choose the movement from which it can expect the greatest measure of social justice."[21]

Barth's socialism was never dogmatic or doctrinaire; he could never take the internal arguments and discussions about its nature with the same seriousness as he would the theological task. This did not in any way undermine its importance for him, but it preserved the crucial eschatological proviso between the kingdom of God and "actually existing socialism" and secured the task of theology as theology, not as disguised sociology or political science.

"Actually Existing Communism"

During the Cold War Barth became notorious in the West for his open attitude toward communist societies. His refusal to join others in condemning the Warsaw Pact invasion of Hungary in 1956 provoked the wrath of many of his previous supporters. Niebuhr's scathing attack on him is well known, as are Brunner's many appeals to him "for leadership at this time."[22]

This openness is the basis of correctly understanding Barth's many criticisms of communism. His attack on Bolshevism, for instance, in the second edition of *Romans* (often quoted to demonstrate Barth's supposed rejection of socialism), must be seen within this context. In the same commentary he can still affirm that Christianity is closer to the "Russian Man" than "his Western counterpart" (p. 463). The danger is, however, that the revolutionary is far more likely to be overcome by evil than the reactionary, because "with his No, he stands so strangely near to God" (p. 480) and therefore is tempted to identify his No with God's No by absolutizing the revolution.

Clearly Barth's rejection of Bolshevism and his critique of communism is not the response of a disillusioned socialist now turned conservative, but that of a disillusioned socialist who has radicalized his socialism by locating it within a more solid theological base, which preserves the "critical distance" necessary for a deabsolutized yet radical praxis.

Between East and West: No Easy Neutrality

Barth's Cold War position "between East and West" has been misunderstood in many ways. It is seen either as a weak kind of neutrality, reflecting his essential "Swissness," or as a blight on his political judgment that casts fundamental doubts on his theological project as a whole.[23] The inability of these critics to understand what they perceive as Barth's "amazing shift in attitude from Nazism to Communism"[24] arises to a large extent out of their failure to perceive Barth's fundamental and consistent commitment to socialism. Even if perverted in practice by Stalinist communism, in principle it is to be supported over against American capitalism, which has not yet begun to face the fundamental social disorder of the time.

Barth's comment that "communism can be warded off only by a better justice on the part of the Western world"[25] cannot mean (given his attitude toward capitalism) a more liberal capitalist justice, but rather a more radical socialist justice. Barth is thus at one with many socialists of the time who were, and still are, seeking a third, socialist way "between East and West."

The Theological Basis of Barth's Socialism

For Barth, as we have noted, all theology was either explicitly or implicitly political. Accepting this general thesis, we must integrate it with the understanding of the socialist contours of Barth's politics that have already been indicated. What, in other words, is the theological basis of Barth's socialism?

The Development of Barth's Thought: A Continuity of Intention

The developments of Barth's theology are well known and well documented, and in my earlier references to the works of Marquardt and Hunsinger I have indicated the links between them and his political praxis. What follows here is an analysis of the continuity and discontinuity in the theological grounding of his socialism. By carefully analyzing three texts that mark crucial stages in his development, I will demonstrate that through the radical theological discontinuities there is a fundamental *continuity of intention,* namely, a search for an adequate theological grounding for political praxis and therefore for socialist commitment. The three texts are "Jesus Christ and the Movement for Social Justice" (1911), his famous Tambach address of 1919, and "Rechfertegung and Recht" (1939).[26]

In 1911 he stated his intention as follows: "We want to demonstrate the inner connection that exists between what is eternal, permanent and general in modern socialism and the eternal Word of God."[27] This essay is a classic expression of the religious-socialist movement led by Kutter and Ragaz and influenced by the Blumhardts (father and son), which had so profoundly shaped the early Barth. Methodologically, the links he draws between socialism and Jesus' kingdom are parallel and reversible. Thus "Jesus Christ is the movement for social justice and the movement for social justice is Jesus Christ in the present" (p. 19). The *identity* between socialism and the kingdom is unmistakable. The liberal presuppositions of this position are apparent; the relation between God and human beings is merely transferred from the individual to the social.

The epoch-making Tambach lecture represents the first indication of Barth's break with religious socialism. In it one breathes an atmosphere completely different from that of 1911; it is an atmosphere of judgment *(krisis),* of transcendence, of revolution. The hyphens on which Barth had once based his relation between the gospel and socialism, between faith and the world, are now "dangerous short circuits."[28] Where there is no hyphenation, there is no reversal of direction. God and the world are radically separated, the identities of the kingdom and of socialism are shattered. "Where then has the Word of God any available connection with our social life? How do we come to act as if it had?" (p. 277).

Having placed God's No on all human claims to the divine, Barth is left with the problem of how to ground ethical, and hence social, action. Here we rediscover the continuity of intention. Barth recognizes that his radical separation of God and human beings could lead to ethical paralysis, but this was never his intention, which was always to provide "an Archimedean point from which the soul, and with the soul, society is moved" (p. 295). The problem lay in achieving this intention, and here Barth is forced into an almost Platonic cast of ideal and representation (p. 260). The weakness of this position both for his theology and for the theological grounding of ethical action and socialist praxis became apparent to Barth over the next decade, and it was only with his recovery of a genuine christological center and his shift from dialectics to analogy that these problems were overcome.

His 1939 essay begins with words that not only echo but almost repeat those of 1911: "In there, in spite of all differences, an inner and vital connection between the service of God in Christian living . . . and . . . what may be described as a 'political' service of God."[29] But now the same intention is rooted in a theological center that transcends the naive identifications of the Safenwil era and simultaneously overcomes the separation of the dialectical era. The *inner and necessary connection* is now located in Christ and the analogy of faith.

These essays demonstrate the fundamental continuity of intention in Barth's theology amid all the significant changes. In a real sense, his mature theology has turned the full circle back to Safenwil, but with a far stronger and more secure theological base achieved through the use of dialectical separation and analogical integration. What remains is to indicate in more detail the mature theological grounding of this intention.

God

"God Himself and God alone, His Spirit, His Word, are the center, the unequivocal ground and beginning and thus the total secret of Barth's theology."[31] No one who has read *Church Dogmatics* can doubt this statement. Barth was "consumed with a passion for God,"[32] and this passion burns deeply through all his writings. But in asserting this it is necessary to remember a cautionary word Barth never tired of speaking: "The Word, and therefore God Himself, does not exist for us apart from the human-being of Christ" (*CD* I/2, 166). His theme, his passion, was not God in isolation, in lofty and terrifying transcendence, a God to be mystically adored and contemplated. No, his theme was always, and without fail, "God for the world, God for us."[33] There is no contradiction, therefore, in the assertion that Barth's intention in his doctrine of God was theologically to ground his socialist praxis. His passion is both for God and for humanity and, more especially, for the link between this God "who materially transforms all things" and the world that is alienated both from God and within itself.

This he does by holding together with utmost consistency God's being and God's act, God's essence and God's revelation. These can be neither separated nor dissolved into each other. "God is who He is in His work," but "not only in His works" (*CD* II/1, 260). Marquardt is fundamentally correct in saying that Barth's "concept of God" is socially reflected, the transcendence he develops is not metaphysical but eschatological, and the development of his concept of God has been substantially situated in his desire to ground adequately his socialist praxis. How is this demonstrated?

Barth's doctrine of God is fundamentally and consistently trinitarian. Here he lays the basis for his theology that preserves it from becoming anthropology or simply a Feuerbachian, or Marxian, projection. Only a trinitarian concentration on what "God is in Godself," and only then on what God is for humans, could overcome this critique of projection and ideology. But the force of Feuerbach's and Marx's practical critiques also need to be met. Even a God self-sufficient in

Godself could be a God of the status quo, a God who sanctions human alienation, a God whose lofty transcendence is too far removed from the struggle of the poor and dispossessed to transform their situation. But if being and act are inseparable, then this can never happen. The God who loves in Godself is the God who loves in revelation of Godself to humans; the God who is community in Godself becomes the God who establishes and creates community with and among people; the God who is freedom in Godself is freely revealed to humans and creates freedom among them.

This holding together of being and act without allowing them to fuse into one another becomes the heartbeat of Barth's theology, the controlling paradigm for a whole series of parallels that one finds consistently repeated: God's being and God's act; the "two natures" Christology; covenant and creation; theory and praxis; grace and nature; gospel and law; God's kingdom and human struggles for justice; gospel and socialism; justification and justice, and so on. In each of these is a common structure that has its basis in the paradigm of "being and act," in the very nature of God.

We can explicate this paradigm as follows: there is both a separation of the divine and the human and a priority of the divine that does not allow either a confusion or a reversal of the two. This is the limiting dimension of the paradigm. However, there is a unity between them that is unbreakable and yet preserves the distinction and the priority of the former. This is the foundational and creative dimension of the paradigm. Applying this to the parallel of gospel and socialism, the following structure becomes apparent. First, there is a distinction between the gospel and socialism that prevents any form of hyphenation between them. There can be no religious-socialism or Christian politics. Both the gospel and socialism are secured in their respective spheres. The former is not secularized, the latter not sacralized. Second, the gospel has the priority over socialism in the sense that it must control the features of the latter and not vice versa. The gospel is thus the limiting feature of socialism, preventing it from becoming an ideology, something to be believed in. But, third, the gospel and socialism are *held together* in an unbreakable unity that preserves these distinctions. The gospel becomes the basis for socialism and socialism becomes a predicate of the gospel.

How does Barth preserve the unity of these parallels, of God in Godself and of God for the world? In his dialectical period he was forced into an unsatisfactory neo-Platonic linkage where "the idea" is "at the same time the oldest thing in existence," "the divine spark which needs to be rekindled."[34] With the development of his mature theology he discovered a new and more substantial center, the doctrine of the two natures of Christ. Here Christology becomes the controlling paradigm of his theology and provides access to the being-act paradigm at the heart of God.

Chalcedonian Christology: The True Ground of Socialist Praxis

It is in Barth's recovery of the Chalcedonian center of all Christology and, hence, theology, that this paradigm is finally located, and the true ground of socialist praxis is secured. Uncovering the structure of the christological paradigm, the following aspects become clear. First, the two-natures doctrine means that God and humans are distinguished from each other, and God is given priority in the relationship. "The Word became flesh" means that God is truly God, not merely a projection of human desires or a product of human alienation. Here Barth retains the passionate tenor of his earlier works. There is still no talk of a God-human continuum that could be reversed in either direction. His rejection of the Lutheran *"communicato idiomatum"* is part of this process. But it also means that the human remains human, that there can be no talk of divinization of the human person or the sacralizing of human action and struggle. This clearly locates the rejection of religious-socialism, along with all other hyphenated hybrids, within a christological center. The project is ruled out from the start by the distinction of the divine and the human in Christ. Christologically, therefore, there can be no reversal of the relationship between God and humans, a position essential both to repel Feuerbach's attack on God and to make a place for the human as human.

This distinction has political connotations, seen in the analogically parallel twofold determination of humans:

> The correspondence which alone can be considered in this connection cannot and will not mean abolition of the "infinite qualitative difference" between God and man. It is a question of responsibility and therefore of a correspondence in which God and man are in clear and inflexible antithesis. It is a question of displaying the image of God, and not the creation of a second God in human form, or of mixing or changing the human form into the one divine form. . . . Whatever the action demanded of us may be, it will be our action, a human action. It will have to attest and confirm the great acts of God; but it will not be able to continue or repeal them . . . the covenant remains, but there is no development of an identity between God and man. (*CD* II/2, 577, 588)

There is not even an identity that develops christologically; the distinction must be maintained. Obviously this christological model is one-sided in a manner similar to Barth's earlier theocentric theology. What becomes important, in fact central, to the *Church Dogmatics* and Barth's mature theology is the second aspect of the paradigm, the unity of the two natures. Significantly, the words that Barth uses to describe the need for this stress are those already encountered in the 1911 lecture and in the 1938 article already discussed. It is necessary, Barth states, when talking about Christ, to discover *"the inner material connection"* between the divinity of and the humanity in Christ, while not forgetting the "formal parallelism" (*CD* III/2, 217). Clearly if this connection cannot be made adequately, then Barth fails christologically by not being able to affirm the Incarnation, and politically, by failing to ground his praxis in a theological base. Thus, although the distinction between the two natures must never be forgotten, the focus must be on the nature of the unity, an understanding of the Incarnation.

Here Barth introduces the crucial link. Humanity and divinity in Christ are not held together by an *analogia entis,* but by an *analogia relationis* (*CD* III/2, 219). It is an analogy of the relationship of love within the inner divine being that is repeated and reflected in the person of Jesus in his being for humanity:

> Jesus lives *kata theon,* after God. As a man He exists *analogously* to the mode of existence of God. In what he thinks and wills and does, in His attitude there is a correspondence, a parallel in the creaturely world to the plan and purpose and work and attitude of God. (*CD* IV/2, 166; my emphasis)

This is important. It lays the christological foundations of the analogical method of holding together God and humans that allows the greatest harmony without identity. It therefore both limits and grounds the relationship. It prevents, for instance, religious-socialism (or Christian-nationalism) and yet allows the grounding of socialist praxis as a human struggle as an analogy of the struggle of God in and for his kingdom. The Christian community is therefore "now free for unqualified participation in the cause of God and *therefore* in the cause of the world of men" (*CD* IV/3, 248; my emphasis).

Conclusion

We cannot reduce Barth's theology to his politics, for it has a dynamic and a power of its own, derived from its object, God, and its source, the Word of God and Christian faith and praxis. Nevertheless, as he himself often stated, all theology has an explicit or an implicit political basis. Barth's politics were socialist, and his theology developed within this context. Barth's political ethics were socialist, and given his ethical method of deriving all from God's command, God's command is therefore socialist. But God's command cannot be divorced from God's being; it is not merely derived from natural law or philosophy. So, clearly, God is, in some form, socialist! Theology in all its contours must therefore reflect this, without reducing it all to this. Further, God's command is not directly translatable into the political arena; socialism has an independent life of its own and is, in its modern form, a recent phenomenon. What exists, therefore, is a socialist tendency in God that must be translated analogically into the political arena in whatever form best fits the time and circumstances.

The echoes of Safenwil are apparent but are now integrated into a christological center that protects the gospel from reduction or confusion and the human from divinization, while maintaining and securing their indivisible relationship. God and humans are bound together in the struggle for humanity, for human liberation, the ultimate ground and goal of human existence, which is achieved in the freedom created by God who loves in freedom. The human project of socialism can thus be affirmed as the particular command of God, taken up by the Christian community in solidarity with the secular, in the power of the freedom of God's liberating Spirit. The Christian community as the "vanguard" of this struggle affirms at once the priority of God and the primacy of the human with no conflict, no separation, and no confusion.

Theology and Violence

Alan Brews

Any theological inquiry in the South African context must take seriously the questions relating to the violence of the prevailing situation. Karl Barth, in his theological response to the issues of war and resistance to tyranny, presents some useful perspectives in this regard.

Barth worked out his attitude toward violence in the context of resistance to Nazism within Germany and World War II. A leading figure of the German church struggle, Barth sought to reject the theological legitimation of Hitler's policies by his involvement in the so-called Faith Movement of German Christians. Central to Barth's theology was a radical allegiance to Jesus Christ, who as the revelation of the wholly other God calls all human activities and systems into question. Only God is absolute. Only God's command is to be obeyed. All human authority is, by implication, relative. The Barmen Declaration of 1934, largely the work of Barth, theologically declares the limits of human authority and the absolute sovereignty of the Word of God, Jesus Christ:

> Jesus Christ, as he is testified to us in the Holy Scripture, is the one Word of God, whom we are to hear, whom we are to trust and obey in life and death. We repudiate the false teaching that the church can and must recognise yet other happenings and powers, images and truths as divine revelation alongside this one Word of God, as the source of her preaching.[1]

We shall consider here Barth's statements on war and forcible resistance in terms of three central categories: the revolution of God, the relationship between church and state, and the concept of the *Grenzfall*.

The Revolution of God

The revolution of God is posited on what Kierkegaard called the "infinite qualitative distance" between God and humanity. This revolution has three moments. The first is the *thesis,* the human condition of alienation and imperfection. Late in his life Barth referred to the human situation as "the regime of vacillation."[2] This is the arena of human praxis, the status quo. The second moment, the *antithesis,* is the revelation of God in the God-man Jesus Christ. The total otherness of his divine nature deabsolutizes all human actions. This is the basis of God's No to human endeavor. Yet because of Jesus' human nature it is possible to discern God's Yes to humankind in the existential situation. This Yes is the command of God that constitutes the foundation of ethics for Christians. History, then, being the locus of the No and Yes of God and the arena for the encounter between God and humanity, becomes the realm of both potential judgment and salvation. The third moment, the original and final *synthesis,* is the kingdom of God, the eschatological motivation that inspires the continuing quest for hope among the possibilities of hope. This synthesis is historically disclosed in Jesus of Nazareth and is the basis of God's perpetual revolution. The dialectic between the thesis and antithesis must continue until this final synthesis is reached.[3]

Although this revolution is perpetuated for the benefit of all humanity, Jesus' life, actions, and death define the perspective from which God commands. Barth describes Jesus as "this poor man, as this (if we may risk the dangerous word) partisan of the poor, and finally this revolutionary."[4] God does not stand impartially in the midst of human conflict. God chooses sides. Barth once again reminds us:

> God stands at every time unconditionally and passionately on this and only this side: always against the exalted and for the lowly, always against those who already have rights and for those from whom they are robbed and taken away.[5]

This was Barth's consistent position from the early days of his commentary on Romans.[6] Undoubtedly the historical content of the categories "lowly" and "poor" must be determined anew within each society. It is here that social analysis becomes implicit in Barth's method and essential to the revolution of God.

Five matters arising from the revolution of God concern us in this essay. First, the real question for Barth is not whether violence is ever *legitimate* but whether God ever *commands* a violent course of action.

It is, after all, God's revolution. This question raises the issue of the relationship between God's revolution and human revolution.

Second, arising from this, all human revolution must be seen in the light of the revolution of God for the Christian. Human revolution can never be more than a response to God's No and Yes in Jesus Christ. The revolution of God thus sets the limit to all human revolution as well as limits to the authority of the existing order. Barth in fact insists that the revolutionary is in greater danger of God-denying Titanism than the reactionary precisely "because with his No he stands so strangely near to God."[7] The revolution loses its legitimacy when it ceases to participate in the judgment of God and takes his judgment into its own hands. It is "zeal for the honor of God" that makes imperative the revolt of the true revolutionary:

> Rebellion and resistance against the regime of vacillation are necessary. It is the command of the hour, of every hour. This command is issued to Christians in the time between the times, and we have to obey it. Zeal for the honor of God means holy and resolute marching off in that direction. It means revolt.

Human participation in the revolution of God is nonetheless a humble task. God will ultimately "overthrow the regime of vacillation." Human beings are to resist and rebel within this assurance:

> But to rise up in rebellion against the regime . . . is something that is humanly possible, that we can do. It is the action that is commanded of us on our allotted path.[8]

Third, the emphasis on the continuous nature of the revolution of God means that the revolution must, at all costs, be perpetuated. The status quo must always be more or less radically negated. The question arises: Can violence be a means God uses to perpetuate *this* revolution?

Fourth, because the revolution is God's alone, nothing else can be granted absolute status. God alone is absolutely free, and all human freedom derives from his freedom. All our statements, theological formulations, and actions can do no more than point to God's absolute reality. For this reason, despite the compelling nature of pacifism as an absolute principle, Barth finally rejects it. Indeed it would be inconsistent with his basic theological assumptions to advocate absolute pacifism or any other ethical absolute. For Barth God alone is absolute. We are to hear and obey God's command, and God, if God is truly God, must be free to command over and beyond absolutized human formulations. It is the supremacy and freedom of this God in Jesus that the church must proclaim.

Fifth, human revolution must have as its purpose and perspective the decision of God to side with the poor and lowly. Human revolution is ultimately a participation in God's concern to "establish justice for the innocent who are threatened and the poor, the widows, the orphans and the strangers who are oppressed."[9] Through an analysis of the existential context of resistance the categories "poor" and "lowly" will receive specific definition.

Church and State

In the light of God's revolution it is evident that the Christian can never be content with the existing order and that the church will always be engaged in resisting the status quo that the state seeks to uphold. In proclaiming Jesus Christ as sovereign Lord the church announces the negation of the existing state in the interests of the true state. To do this the church must simply be the church: it must proclaim the supremacy and freedom of the Word of God.

The submission to the state enjoined in Romans 13:1-7 only applies insofar as the state legitimately uses its God-given authority. God is never bound to any particular form of government and may at "any moment call any of them into question, either in part or as a whole."[10] The church is then called by God to participate in God's No in resisting the state. This resistance is not, however, anarchy. It is in fact the highest service the church can render the state, namely, to oppose the perverted state in the interests of restoring true government. Responsibility does not end with this negation of the prevailing political order; it is the initial step toward a positive process of sociopolitical reconstruction. It is the No for the sake of the Yes.

The church's proclamation also has the positive function of accepting joint responsibility, with the state, as it "participates—on the basis of and by belief in the divine revelation—in the human search for the best or 'most fitting' political system."[11] It must search with the state for a political system that is analogous to the kingdom of God. The foundation of the state for which the church searches is, for Barth, *justice* and not force or order. Force is always a servant of justice if it is used at all. The church may not, therefore, allow the state to subvert the ends of justice in the interests of order. The "tyranny of order" must be resisted by the proclamation of divine justification, which takes the form of justice in political life. It is this justice as the concrete form of divine justification that will both prevent submission from becoming *the tyranny of order* and ensure that resistance does not become "self-justifying rebellion that ends in the *tyranny of anarchy*."[12] The search for justice in a particular situation thus gives concrete form to the revolution of God.

The church cannot give up this search until the final eschatological rule of God is realized. In order to perpetuate the search it must constantly call into question the existing order. This is even more imperative when the state has become tyrannical and has lost its legitimacy as was the case in Nazi Germany where the state had far exceeded the bounds of its authority. For Barth, the oath it demanded of its citizens conflicted with his allegiance to Jesus Christ. In other words, it required an obedience reserved for God alone. Theologically, the state did not have the *authority* to prescribe the oath and Barth did not have the *freedom* to obey it. Resistance to this oath cost Barth his professorship and residence in Germany. Further, in Barth's perspective, the Nazi state had become a radical enemy of Jesus Christ by persecuting the Jews.

Under these circumstances in 1938 Barth evoked the Scottish Confession to resist the state. Article 14 of the confession, which calls on Christians to "save the lives of innocents, to represse tyrannie, and to defend the oppressed," commanded resistance against Nazism: "according to the Scottish confession, under certain conditions there may be a *resistance* to the political power, which is not merely allowed but enjoined by God."[13] Barth insisted that the issue of force could not be avoided by those who live in this world: "Let us be quite clear, by obeying the political order in accordance with God's command, we have in any case directly or indirectly a share in the exercise of force.[14] This is even true when the way of "passive participation" in the prevailing political system is chosen. Passive participation can never be neutrality. As a provisional acceptance of the order of the state under the command of God, it implies an acceptance of co-responsibility for what exists and a commitment to obedience when God requires resistance. Responsibility for violence in a situation cannot be avoided by anyone involved. Here Barth recognizes that in an already violent situation, no one can claim neutrality. All participate, either consciously or unconsciously, in some form of violence.

All states are constantly liable to assert themselves against God rather than obediently seek to establish a community that reflects God's justice. This was particularly the case, in an extreme way, in Germany during the time of Hitler and is similarly true of the apartheid regime in South Africa. The question is not *must we resist,* but *what form must resistance take?* Are there any conditions under which the revolution of God may require the church to engage in violent resistance?

The *Grenzfall*[15]

With this in mind, we need to look at the concept of the *Grenzfall*, which, in Barth's theology, is the idea that God is free to command in a way that may appear to conflict with previous commands. Barth's assumption is that the *content* of the command of God is usually reasonably discernible and universally valid. However, certain exceptional cases exist in which obedience may be required to commands, issuing from the freedom of God, which differ from normal commands. In this *Grenzfall* situation the actual context of Christian praxis becomes vital, even determinative. The *Grenzfall* cannot be considered hypothetically. It refers to the particular command of God in a specific situation. This is also the major difficulty with the *Grenzfall* ethic: By what criteria do we decide that a *Grenzfall* has arisen? What analytical tools do we use to understand the situation in which God commands? We will return to this issue later. For Barth, though, the question of violence is a *Grenzfall*. He would insist that we cannot tackle questions relating to violence apart from the social location of that violence.

Barth's understanding of the respect for human life is critical to this discussion. For Barth, human freedom to live is always within the context of the freedom of God. Life is to be respected "as a divine loan."[16] This respect is created by the command of God especially as revealed in the incarnation of Jesus Christ. However, Barth continues to insist that "life is no second God, and therefore the respect due to it cannot rival the reverence owed to God."[17] To elevate respect for life to an absolute principle approaches a kind of idolatry. This reservation concerning respect for life, however, must always be formulated as "an *ultima ratio,* an exceptional case *(Grenzfall)*." Barth further clarifies:

> Recollection of the superior wisdom, goodness and controlling power of God, and the recollection of the future life, cannot then form a pretext or excuse for attitudes and modes of action in which man may actually evade what is commanded within these limits. They are frontiers that are necessarily set by God and cannot be claimed as emancipations of man. This will be best understood by those who do not treat respect for life as a principle set up by man.[18]

Although Barth's arguments (and largely his praxis) closely

bordered on pacifism, he had to allow for the extreme case in which respect for and preservation of life demands that it be terminated. The possibility of this *Grenzfall* can never be taken lightly, but it cannot be excluded.[19]

The Grenzfall *of War*

War, for Barth, fell into the category of a *Grenzfall* situation. Faced with the tyranny of Hitler, Barth was compelled to consider the possibility of war against Germany as an *ultima ratio*. Between the years 1938 and 1942 he wrote letters to Christians in Czechoslovakia, France, Holland, Britain, and the United States, urging them to take up the struggle against Germany in the interests of restoring a true state within Germany.

Stoesz identifies two dominant themes in these letters that have relevance for our discussion.[20] First, Barth regards war against Germany as a "righteous cause." This theme is dominant in the letters and emphasizes the Yes aspect of the revolution of God. The sociohistorical reason for Barth's emphasis on the Yes at this time was probably the *lack* of effective resistance against Germany by the countries addressed. The contextual need was not theological caution but a cry for help on behalf of the victims of Hitler's oppression.

Theologically the significance of the resurrection of Jesus is central to this theme. Having chastised the French for "eschatological defeatism" and for using the cross as a way to "co-operate today," Barth emphasized the proclamation of the "risen Christ 'as the King, whose Kingdom has no boundaries' and who 'has overcome the world.'" It was the Yes of God in the resurrection that became the primary motivation for resistance against Hitler. Participation in the war could thus be seen as participation in the revolution of God against all human arrogance. The resurrection meant that evil was already defeated and therefore had no ontological existence as such. "Evil remained 'real' only in the sense that it was a shadow of the good." For this reason Barth could speak of the war as "a beneficent, a merciful thing, which is in the truest interest of even those most directly affected thereby." It was possible to engage in the war with "good conscience" as long as it was understood that the war being waged *against* Germany was also being waged *for* Germany.

Furthermore, the war was a corrective action, and as such a sign of the grace of God. War as judgment and war as an act of love were not separated, and love remained primary. This positive relationship between love and judgment is critical to our understanding of the issues of war and violence. Judgment is not the vindictive act of a cruel God, but the gracious act of a loving God in the interests of those being judged and of all humanity. If the *ultima ratio* of war or violence is ever commanded by God it is only as a manifestation of grace and never as divine retribution.

The second theme in Barth's war letters is that war is the judgment of God. This is evident in the qualifications placed on the assertion that war is a "righteous cause." In his characteristic dialectic manner he refused to make a direct connection between divine justification and human justice. Here we hear the No of the cross that corresponds to the Yes of the resurrection. The church was to continue to proclaim her own message of justification, even to Hitler and the rest of Germany. The war could not simply be equated with the task of the church or the revolution of God. The human struggle for justice cannot directly reflect divine justification—it can only point toward it. The guilt of all nations implicit in the failure of the Versailles Treaty to prevent the eventuality of World War II was to be recognized. The failure of all nations to take responsibility for the war led Barth to insist that although "Germany was guilty of starting the war, the other nations were guilty of avoiding the war." Thus, all nations came under God's judgment.

The recognition of the war as a righteous cause did not mean that it was automatically God's cause. The judgment of God also applied in the sense that the righteous cause of the war was not to be seen as a legitimation of all Allied actions. War was always a "dreadful ultimate instrument" used to correct intransigent injustice. The suffering created by war also falls under the judgment of God. Barth insisted that suffering and resistance were inseparable within the confession of Jesus Christ. He insisted that suffering was not ontologically good, but that the acceptance of suffering was unavoidable in the process of resistance.

The No of the cross receives greater emphasis in Barth's postwar systematic writings. He begins the section on war in *Church Dogmatics* III/4 with a radical debunking of the myths about war. Further, he exposes the confusion of nationalistic and racial arrogance with the cause of justice and freedom. Barth describes war as a fundamental struggle for the acquisition of economic power motivated by material selfishness. He concludes:

> We to-day, unlike previous generations, are not merely qualified but compelled and certainly summoned to face the reality of war without any optimistic illusions. How unequivocally ugly war now is![21]

War can never be an *opus proprium* of the state; it is always an *opus alienum*. This option can be considered only as a last resort. War is an extreme *Grenzfall* question:

> All affirmative answers to the question are wrong if they do not start with the assumption that the inflexible negative of pacifism has almost infinite arguments in its favour and is almost overpoweringly strong.[21]

Perhaps the most compelling point Barth makes concerning the *Grenzfall* of war is that the real issue is not war nor violence, but peace. "A peace that is no real peace can make war inevitable." The true purpose of the *opus alienum* of war is a "just peace."[23] This relates to our discussion on the use of forcible resistance. The *telos* of the forcible resistance must be liberation based on justice. Only in this sense can the human praxis of war or forcible resistance, by analogy, point to the praxis of God.

The final consideration under the *Grenzfall* of war is the responsibility of the individual toward the state when the *ultima ratio* of war is discerned. Barth firmly rejects the "illusory distinction between individual and social ethics"[24] and insists that because the question of war has been addressed to the state it is the concern of each individual within the state. The individual, as citizen, must respond as one whose "obedience to the command of God means also that he must think and speak and act and pray with and for the state."[25] State decisions do not absolve individuals of responsibility or guilt. In taking seriously his or her obedience to God the individual Christian may have to resist the existing state in the interests of the true state. This means that there can be no uncritical acceptance of conscription or participation in the violence of the state. The whole of humanity collectively and each individual separately stands under the judgment of God. God's command is supreme. Presumably the same argument applies to those who participate in forcible resistance. Ultimately it is not the commands of the liberation movement that call the individual to action but rather the command of God.

The Grenzfall *of Forcible Resistance*

One consequence of the *Grenzfall* ethic, particularly significant for the South African context, is the rejection of the option of a blanket condemnation of all forms of violence. Barth would regard this attitude as a failure to confront the real issues by depending on an absolute principle independent of the "wholly other" God. For some, nonviolence has become an idol. This commitment to nonviolence, born of a fear of the consequences of violence, has paralyzed the South African churches' ability to respond with viable, active programs of resistance. The contradiction is that these same churches continue, even if by default, to support conscription into the South African armed forces. In his commentary on the Scottish Confession, Barth establishes the necessity for resistance and refuses to exclude the possibility of forcible resistance:

> This may not only be passive resistance but an active one, a resistance which can in certain circumstances be a matter of opposing *force* by force. . . . It may be that the repressing of tyranny and the prevention of the shedding of innocent blood can be carried out in no other way.[26]

Remembering the unavoidable, direct or indirect share in the exercise of force, Barth shows the absurdity of excluding the option of forcible resistance in an already violent situation.

> Whether the repressing of tyranny will be a matter of forcible resistance or not, is not something that can be decided in advance. But active resistance as such cannot and may not be excluded out of fear of the ultima ratio of forcible resistance. And the possible consequence of forcible resistance may certainly not be excluded in advance.[27]

Barth, writing just before the outbreak of war in 1938, hopes that the *ultima ratio* of forcible resistance may be averted. The church or the individual Christian, however, may never pray to be spared "obedience to God in this worldly sphere either, to be spared the political service of God as such."[28] No refuge from political responsibility can be found in absolute principles. To seek such refuge is to deny both God and human dignity. Refuge from the demands of the gospel cannot be found in the gospel itself! God is free, in the name of divine revolution, to command forcible resistance. The church and Christians are free in Jesus Christ to obey. In fact, it is only when the church has been liberated from fear of the *ultima ratio* of forcible resistance that it becomes free to explore realistically the nonviolent options for resistance in a given situation.

After the Second World War in 1946 Barth expressed himself even more strongly when considering the relationship between the civil community and the Christian community. Here he insists that in extreme cases it may even be the responsibility of the church not only to support and approve of but to *suggest* "the violent solution of conflicts in the political community."[29] Clearly, however, such forcible resistance is to be regarded as an extraordinary course of action.

The revolution of God cannot and must not be subverted. The ruling passion of Barth's theology and praxis is that God must be free to be God. That is, when a situation presents us with the dilemma of having to choose between the maintenance of order and the struggle for justice, we must seek justice even at the risk of order.

Barth, Violence, and South Africa

Jürgen Moltmann makes the point that Barth's ethic is essentially a discipleship ethic. It presupposes a level of Christian commitment because its foundation is the humanity of God in Jesus Christ:

> Christocratic ethics can only be discipleship ethics. It is ethics for Christians but not Christian ethics for the state. It is political ethics of the Christian community but not Christian politics of the civil community.[30]

In many contexts this would constitute a criticism of the Barthian approach. In the South African context it is precisely this critique that compels us to reread Barth.

The current South African situation is theologically similar to the church struggle in Germany in that the self-understanding of oppressed and oppressor emerges to some extent from the Judeo-Christian tradition. This type of context calls for a discipleship ethic. Barth's approach makes its greatest contribution where divergent voices claim divine legitimation for their political programs. Thus, we need to look at how Barth helps us to struggle with the reality of violence in South Africa.

First, he places beyond reach the refuge of nonviolence as an absolute principle. The paralysis of praxis evident in many churches and among Christians largely results from fear of the *ultima ratio* of violence (forcible resistance). Insistence upon the freedom of God and thus the relativity of all human freedom shifts the attention from human formulations to God's command. While recognizing the positive appeal of pacifism, we may not idolize it. It, like life, is not a second God.

Second, violence as war or forcible resistance may be commanded by God as an *ultima ratio* in a given context. Only those who have seriously struggled with the compelling arguments for pacifism are in a position to recognize the moment in which the *ultima ratio* applies. After decades of thwarted passive resistance many South Africans have been forced by the realities of an increasingly repressive situation to accept that the conditions for that *ultima ratio* have been realized. Following Barth we must reckon with the possibility that it is these reluctant revolutionaries who may have heard God most clearly. In any case we cannot reject their option for armed struggle as un-Christian. It *could* be the most Christian option possible.

Third, the *ultima ratio* of violence is always an *opus alienum,* whether it be undertaken by the state, a liberation movement, or an individual. Since violence is always a "dreadful ultimate instrument," we should consider the option of violence under the judgment of the "wholly other" God.

Fourth, violent resistance can be advocated only as a participation in the revolution of God. It is thus always subject to the higher authority of "Jesus Christ as attested to in the Scriptures and the Confessions of the Reformation."[31] In this regard Yoder notes the "distinctively Christian note" in Barth's approach, indicating that under the revolution of God violent resistance must be undertaken "without regard for its effectiveness."[32] Consequently, the use of violence must reflect the intention of God. All Christian action must point to the love of God in Jesus Christ for all humanity and be oriented toward the realization of justice as the concrete form of love in history. Violent resistance can only be "good" when it is undertaken for the benefit of all, even the enemy. It must seek to establish a justice that will serve all, in our case all South Africans. This issue causes the Christian constantly to weigh the cost of violence in the interests of the humanization of the struggle for liberation. The injunction to "love your enemies" can be properly understood only in this light. Christian praxis, even if it may contain violence, should have the best interests of the enemy at heart. In the *Grenzfall* situation it is possible for violence to be an affirmation of love rather than its negation. Consequently, the violence that enemies perceive as directed *against* them is actually *for* them. Yet violence can never be "good" in an absolute sense. It may, however, in the midst of an imperfect world, point to the goodness of God. The violence of the state, which amounts to the forcible imposition of an order devoid of justice and peace contrary to the good of the majority of people, does not reflect the intention of God. It may even be argued that in the long term such violence contradicts the interests of the oppressors. It is the repression of tyranny that the Scottish Confession commends as a "good work before God." The real issue is, therefore, not violence but resisting the tyranny of illegitimate government in the interests of true government. Violent resistance may be commanded by God as an instrument to establish justice.

Finally, in the midst of the diverse forms of violence in South Africa, the Barthian approach demands that all accept responsibility.

No one is innocent. The individual's task as a citizen makes consideration of his or her role in the existing conflict imperative. Confronted by the many forms of violence in the situation, the Christian must decide which one bears closest analogy to the revolution of God. Unfortunately, Barth does not provide adequate tools for the analysis of violence in society in order to facilitate such decisions.

Cautions

Barth's understanding of violence is not, however, without limitations. As we have mentioned, his ethics are discipleship ethics. We have recognized both the weakness and the strength of this reality. Three further cautions apply to a Barthian approach to the issue of violence in South Africa.

First, the interpretation of violence as a righteous cause can easily be misused. The righteous cause, based on the resurrection, could become a crusade that does not responsibly account for the guilt and suffering of humanity implicit in the theology of the cross. In his systematic postwar writings, Barth posits a clear dialectic between violence as a righteous cause and violence as the judgment of God. We must live with this dialectic in this "time between the times."

Second, the question arises as to whether violence can ever be undertaken in good conscience. Were the American commentators on Barth's war letters more realistic in insisting that war at least be fought "without the benefit of conscience" or even "with a bad and tortured conscience for the sins that have brought us to this tragic necessity of fighting"?[33] Ultimately we may be able to justify our actions before humanity, but before God we remain guilty. Although this emphasis is not entirely absent in his theology, Barth's critics must be affirmed. Human action is always provisional and relative. It is thus threatened with failure and disobedience to the command of God at every moment. Bonhoeffer insists that the acceptance of guilt is a consequence of the free responsibility of humanity:

> When a man takes guilt upon himself in responsibility, and no responsible man can avoid this, he imputes this guilt to himself and to no one else; he answers for it; he accepts responsibility for it. He does not do this in the insolent presumptuousness of his own power, but he does it in the knowledge that his liberty is forced upon him and that in this liberty he is dependent upon grace. Before other men the man of free responsibility is justified by necessity; before himself he is acquitted by his conscience; but before God he hopes only for mercy.[34]

Guilt before the No of God is as necessary as affirmation before the Yes of God. Nonetheless, anxiety about the judgment of God must not paralyze human praxis. God says No in order to say Yes!

The third caution is most significant. Barth's theology constantly takes social analysis for granted but neither emphasizes the need for that analysis nor provides viable models for analysis. The *Grenzfall* situation, in particular, requires social analysis. Barth does not give specific answers to such questions as: What are the criteria by which a *Grenzfall* situation is recognized? How does the Christian discern the point at which God commands the use of violence? How does the Christian choose between the *violences* in an already violent context? The simple answer, for Barth, is that the command of God must be heard. Yet this hearing always occurs in a specific context. The situation will influence the praxis of Christians. The question still applies: How do we understand the situation? More specifically, accepting Barth, how do we understand the situation from the perspective of the poor?

This defines the difference between Barth and contextual theologians. The *Grenzfall,* which Barth sees as an exceptional case, is his image for contextual theology. Contextual theology, however, insists that the whole of life is a *Grenzfall* situation. The *Grenzfall* for the contextual theologian is the norm. But the nature of the Third World and oppressive situations in which contextual theologies are being written is such that the exception *is* the norm. Thus the contextual theologians have been forced by their method to develop adequate skills for social analysis.

The critical questions relating to discernment of the conditions under which God commands forcible resistance can be answered only by adequate social analysis. Liberation theologians have sought to respond to this dilemma in their quest for sociological models of analysis. There is no way around analysis. It is imperative that theologians search for tools to aid in the analysis of the context of Christian praxis. There are two poles in dialectic tension with one another in the consideration of violence by Christians. The first, firmly established by Barth, is the supremacy of God. The second, recognized by Barth but emphasized by contextual theologians, is the specific context of humanity. Neither can be neglected. It is the knowledge of the revolution of the wholly other God in Jesus Christ that defines the *content* of human action. Analysis of the human context will define the *form* human action must take in obedience to the command of God. The freedom of God establishes the possibility of violence as an *ultima ratio*, and social analysis gives flesh and blood to that possibility in a given social context.

The real question is this: Which model of social analysis is to be used in theology and how is this social analysis to become a constitutive moment in theological reflection?[35] Liberation theologians have generally opted for the Marxist model of social analysis—not because of an ideological commitment to Marxism (and often in criticism of it), but because it is, in their view, the most useful model for understanding society from the side of the poor and oppressed.

Romans 13:
A Hermeneutic
for Church and State

C. A. *Wanamaker*

Not surprisingly in light of his subsequent fame as the theologian of
the Word of God, Barth's initial notoriety was based on a biblical
commentary of that most Protestant of books, Paul's Epistle to the Romans. Disillusioned by the support many of his former theological
teachers had given to Kaiser Wilhelm's war ideology at the start of the
First World War, Barth was convinced that they had failed ethically
and therefore their dogmatic and exegetical presuppositions were
grossly incorrect.[1] As a result he determined to go back to basics in the
form of biblical exegesis and interpretation. In this essay I propose to
examine one specific theme in Barth's biblical interpretation, namely,
the question of church and state. In what follows I will look at three
distinct stages in Barth's understanding of this problem through his
exegesis and interpretation of the classic New Testament passage on
this theme, Romans 13:1-7. By doing so I will show Barth's changing
method of interpreting Scripture and how this affected his changing
understanding of the church-state question. In the final section I will
attempt to suggest how Barth might have viewed the contemporary
South African situation in light of his definitive interpretation of Romans 13:1-7.

The Divine Revolution

The interpretations Barth offers of Romans 13 in the first and second
editions of his commentary differ dramatically and therefore must be
considered separately. However, before we begin our examination of

Barth's interpretation of Romans 13.1-7 in the first edition of *Romans*,[2] we must take a brief look at his exegetical method.

Barth's approach to the Bible was already taking shape in 1916 after his fundamental rejection of liberal theology. In a well-known lecture given that year, Barth spoke of "the strange new world within the Bible."[3] It was strange because what he had been taught to treat as a document about humankind's religious quest for God he discovered to be "the Word of God." By this he meant that "it is not the right human thoughts about God which form the content of the Bible, but the right divine thoughts about men."[4] This strange new world challenged all forms of human religious practice and the sovereignty of human reason upon which they were based.[5] This world could be grasped only when God was recognized as the true and final cause of the history contained in the Bible.[6] Underlying this viewpoint was Barth's increasing dissatisfaction with the methods of contemporary theology as applied to the study of the Bible. Rejecting the historical method as the key to interpreting the Bible, he claimed that the "Holy Scriptures will interpret themselves" to those who seek with faith to understand them.[7]

His new understanding of the Bible heralded a radical departure from the prevailing liberal theology of the time and led to the first edition of *Romans,* which appeared in 1919. In the preface Barth declared that the purpose of the historical-critical method of biblical exegesis was to show that the differences between Paul's time and the present were "purely trivial." His whole effort in interpretation, he stated, was directed toward seeing "through and beyond history into the spirit of the Bible" because he believed that the problems the Christians of his day confronted were the same problems Paul had confronted. Therefore Paul's answers could provide illumination for contemporary Christians.[8] Not surprisingly, then, the reader finds in the commentary absolutely no attempt at traditional exegesis, as Barth's understanding of Scripture at this time made such activity unnecessary. He accepted that his problems were Paul's problems and that his task was to interpret what Paul was saying directly to him and to his contemporaries.[9]

Reading Romans 13:1-7 with its emphatic demand that the Christian should be in subjection to the ruling powers troubled Barth. When the commentary was written Barth was in his most radical socialist phase; his thoughts about God, eschatology, and ethics were strongly influenced by socialist revolutionary understanding. Marquardt has shown that Barth was in dialogue with the revolutionary writings of Lenin at the time and that his fundamental position was that of revolutionary anarchy, which he saw as part of the revolutionary process leading toward the kingdom of God in the material world.[10] To avoid the traditional interpretation of the text, which in effect called for Christians to be good, compliant citizens without reference to the character of the state, Barth introduced a unique interpretation. He claimed that Paul intended Romans 12:21 to serve as a kind of heading over what follows in 13:1-7 and therefore was directed to the Christian's relation with the state. This verse, which in any usual reading of the text functions as the conclusion to Romans 12:14-20, enabled Barth to place a powerful reservation beside the traditional interpretation of the passage, because when read with 13:1ff. it led to the assumption that the state was evil.

In his exposition of the passage, Barth argues that the state in the current world is founded upon power and coercion, in contrast to the righteousness and freedom of God's eschatological state. Because evil has power on earth, any power not caused by the new relation between God and humankind established by Jesus Christ is of necessity evil, and this means that "the power of the state in the present is diametrically opposed to the purpose of God."[11] According to Romans 12:21 Christians must not be overcome by evil, and since Barth argues for the essential and inevitable evil nature of states as they exist in the real world, Christians can "have nothing to do with the power of the state," and it should never occur to them "to want to preserve or strengthen it."[12] Barth's revolutionary anarchist tendencies are clearly in evidence here.

Even when he acknowledges the main teaching of the passage concerning subjection to the state, he immediately qualifies it by maintaining that in Christ the Christian "does not recognize the superiority of the state" because it "has now already fallen"; therefore the Christian "will never be able to be a subject, a citizen, a kinsman of a nation or a party . . . with real emotion."[13] Behind this lies Barth's emphasis on the eschatological dimension of Christian existence, which had been totally lacking in the dominant liberal theology of the day. The eschatological commitment of Christians to the kingdom of God provides one of the fundamental reasons why they can have nothing to do with the present political order, according to Barth. As a result of their future expectation they must "concentrate on the absolute revolution of God and give up on the whole sphere of penultimates (which this world constitutes) to the process of dissolution."[14]

Barth recognizes that the state is not without claims on the Christian, but he makes a careful distinction between what the state can legitimately demand of the Christian and what is beyond its competence. He understands Romans 13:7 as an expression of the absolute limits placed on the demands the state can make on the Christian. The state can require taxes, tribute, respect, and honor, but Barth insists that the Christian must not go one step further. The Christian's obligation ends whenever the demands of the state threaten to compromise God, and they must be resisted at that point. As Barth sees it, the Christian can accept "no combination of throne and altar, no Christian patriotism, no disposition towards democratic crusades," all of which would represent a betrayal of the gospel. This, however, does not require an otherworldly withdrawal nor does it even legitimate such a flight, because in the same breath Barth can say, "Strikes and general strikes and street fighting if there must be, but no religious justification and glorification for it."[15]

We can now make several observations about Barth's scriptural interpretation in general and of Romans 13:1-7 in the first edition of *Romans*. First, he makes absolutely no attempt to engage the world of Paul. It is as though Paul had written the letter in 1919 and Barth simply offered a running commentary on the issues raised by it. For him there is no difference between Paul's problems and his own; they become in Barth's interpretation the same problems. Second, his linking of Romans 12:21 to Romans 13:1-7 is ingenious in that it allows him on the one hand to identify the state as an evil institution and on the other to provide a fundamental limitation of the Christian's obligation to the state since the Christian must not allow himself or herself to be overcome by the state as an evil power. Third, Barth consistently maintains a radical revolutionary stance. At one point he even insists that Christianity is more radical than Leninism since it has an "all or nothing" attitude in connection with the kingdom of God.[16]

The Negation of Legitimism and Revolution

By 1920 Barth's thought had developed to the extent that it was clear to him that a new edition of *Romans* was necessary to correct the fundamental flaws of his first attempt. In the first edition he had sought to overturn the whole direction of nineteenth-century theology, which had identified the noblest thoughts and deeds of humans with God. He recognized, however, that he had failed to achieve his goal because he had not been radical enough in maintaining a complete separation between God and man. This problem was particularly acute because he had made too explicit the connection between the kingdom of God and the historical process. Put simply, Barth saw that God could be experienced or defined in terms of revolutionary political activity,[17] but this violated his intention of reasserting the complete sovereignty of God as the basis of theology.

In order to preclude any form of immediacy between God and man, to protect the transcendent sovereignty of God from any form of relationalism in which humanity seeks to approach God through its thoughts or actions, Barth developed his dialectic method.[18] As its name suggests, this method consisted of question and answer, affirmation and negation, thesis and antithesis in a relentless attempt at "gaining illumination from both and thus moving closer to the intangible heart of the matter."[19] At a fundamental level, however, it was essentially negative because it placed all human activity under divine judgment.

When we turn to Barth's exegesis of Romans 13:1-7 we are immediately confronted with the dramatic change he introduced into his interpretation of the passage. No longer does he merely set himself against the evil power of the state that, with its false demands for obedience, claims the power to regulate human activity; he turns radically on the behavior of the revolutionary in order to subject him or her to the claim of God as well. Through his interpretation he tries to establish what he calls the "great negative possibility." Romans 13:1-7, according to Barth, concerns an important negative dimension of Christian ethical behavior. It emphasizes the possibility of "not-doing" something when the inclination is to do something. Elsewhere Barth describes negative ethics as "things not willed and not done" that are "pregnant with parabolic significance, powerful in bearing witness, capable of concentrating attention upon the 'Beyond.'"[20] It needs to be stressed, however, that from Barth's new perspective ethical action or inaction has no direct bearing on bringing about the kingdom of God since this would again confuse the role of the divine and the human. When applied to this passage, Barth seeks to argue that because civil authority provides a demonstration or parable concerning the order of the "Coming World" it must not be broken through. This is precisely what the requirement of subjection in the text tries to ensure.[21] By its very nature this interpretation makes its strongest attack on revolutionaries as those dedicated to breaking through and overturning the existing order.

As in the first version of *Romans,* Barth begins with Romans 12:21 in order to negate the state and civil authority in the presence of the holy and sovereign God. He maintains that the existing civil order is aimed against God and the possibility of his disturbing the normal course of human affairs. Every human government seeks to act as God by daring "to regulate and determine almost all" human behavior, by "requiring obedience and sacrifice as though they had been invested with the authority of God," and by claiming to be the "peace which all men yearn after." For Barth, this "pseudo-transcendence," or playing at being God, demonstrates the evil character of the civil authorities.[22] One can observe the evil that is fundamental to the existing order of governments in those ordinances that assert their objective right over against others, and ultimately against God. From this, revolution, the desire to establish a new right, is born. The tragedy of the revolutionary is that he "stands so strangely near to God" in his rejection of the existing order. He errs by mistaking his own revolutionary activity to establish the new right with the divine revolution in which Jesus Christ "is the true answer to the injury wrought by the existing order." In doing this he is overcome by evil.[23]

How then does one "overcome evil with good" as God requires? Certainly the answer is *not* what Barth calls "legitimism," that is, the principle of accepting the authority of the evil civil powers who rule this world. *This* is a revolt against God just as much as is the revolution of the revolutionary. (Indeed, as is shown in the other essays in this volume, although Barth's bias in favor of the oppressed in their rejection of the status quo was at times obscured by other preoccupations, it remained a decisive characteristic of this theology throughout his life, *ed.*) Barth's immediate solution is to call for a radical return to a "not-doing," which consists in not being angry, not engaging in assault, not demolishing. "This turning back is the ethical factor in the command, *overcome evil with good,*" and it points to God "who wishes to be recognized as He that *overcometh* the unrighteousness of the existing order."[24] This is the real meaning of what is called for in Romans 13:1-7, according to Barth, and for this reason we do not need to follow his exposition of the passage, which simply confirms this.

The change in Barth's interpretation from the first commentary is indeed remarkable and raises important questions. To what extent is the interpretation of Scripture for him anything more than a subjective interpretation, since his experience, his questions, his understanding become a Procrustean bed for the exposition of Romans? To what extent does his interpretation have meaning for us today when our experiences, our questions, and our understandings arc largely different?

In trying to make room for the Bible to be a genuine revelation from God for people in his own time, Barth forgot that it had also been a revelation to people in the first century. In the earliest phase of his interpretation he made the wall between the first century and the twentieth century so transparent that no difference could be detected between the two. In doing so he failed to do justice to Paul as well as to those who made the wall opaque and found only the religion of the past in the Bible without acknowledging that it contained a word of revelation from God for the present. As James D. Smart has observed, Barth

> established his point that exegesis in separation from exposition is futile, and yet the character of his achievement gave warning that exegesis and exposition must remain in tension as well as in union with each other. In short, there must be an ever-renewed dialogue between the interpreter and the text in which the interpreter gives the text freedom to speak with its own unique accents out of its ancient situation.[25]

To some extent, the later Barth learned this lesson, and it is to this phase of his interpretation of Scripture that we now turn.

The Co-opting of the State

In June 1938 Barth published *"Rechtfertigung und Recht"* ("Justification and Justice"), which later appeared in English as *"Church and State."*[26] Looking at the near total capitulation of the church in the face of National Socialism in Germany, and even the failure of the Confessing Church to live up to its own demands, Barth attempted to expound a satisfactory interpretation of the connection between church and state in light of his christocentric theological outlook. Dismissing the views of the Reformers as lacking a proper biblical foundation, and ultimately a true christological one,[27] Barth turned to the New Testament for the necessary scriptural and christological base from which to explicate the connection between the mission of the church in preaching justification by faith and the responsibility of the state in ensuring human justice. The position he formulated in "Church and State" became the basis for "his political statements and actions over subsequent years."[28]

Around 1930, Barth, influenced by his study of Anselm, largely abandoned the dialectic method of theology that had dominated his work from the days of the second edition of *Romans*. In place of its negative tendency to relativize all human experience in the face of the sovereignty of God and divine judgment, he began to employ a much more positive theological method that understood theology as faith seeking rational understanding. His new conception of theology stressed that the Bible as the written Word of God was the major source for understanding the relation between God and the world, between Christ on the one hand and creation and redemption on the other. In other words, "'the infinite qualitative distinction' between

God and man" was replaced by an emphasis "on their *relationship* through God's Word."[29] This new methodological insight laid the foundation for his *Church Dogmatics* (the first volume of which appeared in 1932) as well as for the possibility of a new attempt at interpreting Romans 13:1-7 and the whole question of the connection between church and state.

"Church and State" represents Barth's definitive interpretation of Romans 13:1-7, but it is more than just an exposition of this pivotal text. In it Barth undertook to articulate a fully biblical understanding of the church-state question for the sake of the church in its struggle against Hitler and Nazism. Following the lead of K. L. Schmidt, his New Testament colleague at Basel, Barth begins the main part of his study with an examination of Jesus' confrontation with Pilate, because he sees in it a prototype of the church-state relationship. Nevertheless, this part of the study is largely decorative and peripheral to the main thrust of the essay, and therefore we may pass over it for our purposes.[30]

The main part of the essay is devoted to the study of Romans 13:1-7 and 1 Timothy 2:1-7, from which Barth derives his complex understanding of the relationship between church and state. He first takes up Romans 13:1-7, to explicate "the essence of the state" as a necessary step in determining the relation of the church to the state. In developing his theological understanding of the state, this passage plays a decisive role because his interpretation of it enables him to establish what R. E. Hood describes as Barth's "Christological basis for the state."[31] To achieve this Barth does what was virtually unthinkable in his earlier commentaries on Romans: he constructively employs the results of historical criticism. He begins by noting that the Greek term *exousiai* (powers or authorities) refers to angelic powers or authorities throughout the New Testament and that these angelic powers were thought to be represented in the state, which is described by the same Greek word in Romans 13:1. Just as angelic powers may assume a "demonic" character when they become perverted, Barth argues that the state, as a representative of the angelic powers, can become "demonic"—as it had in the case of Pilate's unjust condemnation of Jesus. He supports this position by referring to various other New Testament texts.[32] But Barth notes another important feature about the angelic powers that is well attested in the New Testament. The destiny of the "demonic" angelic powers is subordination to Christ and through him to God because this was the purpose for which they were created. Since the resurrection these powers have been called to order by Christ as their head and are to serve and glorify him.

The political angelic powers represented in the state are thereby subject to the same necessities and constraints to which the other angelic powers are subject, and thus they too "should serve the Person and the Work of Jesus Christ and therefore the justification of the sinner," since their power derives from and belongs to Christ.[33]

Rather than attempt to demythologize this biblical myth regarding the heavenly world or to explain it in symbolic terms, Barth treats it as a realistic presentation of reality and then relates it to Romans 13:1-7. The subordination of the state to God is clear in Romans 13, Barth finds, because it stresses that all governing authorities come from God, have been instituted by him, and are his servants for good. But in light of his discussion of the angelic powers and their subordination to Christ, Barth argues that God as depicted in Romans 13 cannot be understood apart from the "person and work of Christ"; thus any interpretation that focuses on God under the general rubrics of "Creator and Ruler" must be rejected. Barth goes on to maintain that "when the New Testament speaks of the State, we are, fundamentally, in the *Christological* sphere; we are on a lower level than when it speaks of the church, yet, in true accordance with its statements on the church, we are in the same unique Christological sphere."[34] Thus Barth believes himself to have overcome the inherent weakness of the Reformers' understanding of the state by giving the state, even the "demonic" state, a christological foundation.

Having established that the state, like the church, stands in the christological sphere, Barth next attempts to explain the precise connection between them. He discovers the key in the exhortation to Christians found in 1 Timothy 2:1-7. According to his interpretation, a reciprocal relationship exists between church and state. The church and its members are required to pray for the rulers and high officials of the state that they may discharge their principal duty of ensuring peace and order through the maintenance of human justice. Only when rulers fulfill their divinely appointed task can the church have the freedom and peace necessary to fulfill its mission of preaching justification by faith. Thus the church through its prayers affirms the need for the state to remain legitimate, while the state through the proper exercise of its power guarantees the right of the church to proclaim the gospel of Christ.[35]

Barth believes that 1 Timothy 2:1-7 constitutes the primary exhortation to the church concerning its relation to the state and provides the basis for understanding the command of Romans 13:1 to "be in subjection to the ruling authorities." This subjection can never be absolute and unquestioning because it must always be held in tension with the church's obligation to preach justification. "Thus the subjection required of Christians *cannot* mean that they accept and take upon themselves responsibility for those intentions and undertakings of the State which directly or indirectly are aimed against the freedom of preaching."[36] In fact, Barth insists that not to resist the state when it "has perverted its God-given authority" would be to become enemies of the state by not calling it back to its true character and function, which is to "create and administer justice."[37] For Barth this is the practical side of the church's guarantee of the state through its prayers. In other words, the church cannot simply withdraw from public life and from political responsibility through its prayers for the state. It must actually criticize the state when it defaults in its God-ordained role because the church alone is the basis and preserver of the state. Barth, operating within his christological understanding of the state, means by this that the state's one reason for existing is to provide the context in which the church can carry out its mission of preaching justification by faith; since only the church can know that this is the true basis of the state, it alone can preserve the state when it falls short of its responsibility for establishing and protecting "true human law . . . that is, the law of freedom for the preaching of justification."[38]

Barth's argument regarding the relation between the church and the state is profoundly audacious. By putting the state in the christological sphere, he has turned the tables on every form of civil religion by theologically co-opting the state into the realm of redemption. This has enabled him to define the church's subjection to the state in terms of responsibility for ensuring that the state creates and administers human justice so that the divine justification may be preached without hindrance. As Barth himself put it:

> The Church *must have freedom to proclaim divine justification.* . . .
> This right of the Church to liberty means the foundation, the maintenance, the restoration of everything—certainly of all human law.
> Wherever this right is recognized, and wherever a true church makes the right use of it . . . there we shall find a legitimate human authority and an equally legitimate human independence; tyranny on the one hand, and anarchy on the other, Fascism and Bolshevism alike, will be dethroned; and the true order of human affairs—the justice, wisdom and peace, equity and care for human welfare which are necessary to that true order—will arise.[39]

We need to mention one final detail of Barth's understanding of the church-state relation at this point. Barth recognizes that Romans 13 and other New Testament passages do not answer all of the questions we may pose about the Christian's responsibilities to the state. The New Testament in particular assumes the existence of an authoritarian state and treats Christians only as subjects. This differs considerably, however, from modern democratic states where people are citizens with political rights and duties. "For us," Barth writes, "the fulfilment of political duty means . . . responsible choice of authority, responsible decision about the validity of laws, responsible care for their maintenance, in a word, political action, which may and must also mean political struggle."[40] Clearly Barth's political outlook here is redolent of his views at the time of the first edition of *Romans*. Barth maintains that the idea of passive subjection to the state, as Romans 13 is often understood to teach, is already broken by 1 Timothy 2. The church, according to this latter text, must actively engage in intercession for the state, and serious prayer requires corresponding works. Thus Barth urges that whether Christians pray for the preservation of the just state or that the state will become just, they must commit themselves in thought and action so that their prayers may be fulfilled. But how far can the Christian's political action go? Barth counsels that the Christian must reckon "with the possibility of revolution, the possibility . . . that we may have to 'overthrow with God' those rulers who do not follow the lines laid down by Christ."[41] Without accepting this possibility the Christian can be true neither to the ideal of the democratic state that Barth maintains is the New Testament's conception of the state nor to the mission of the church that insists upon the right to preach divine justification. This affirmation ultimately places Barth on the side of the oppressed and the revolutionary over against the oppressors who seek to maintain the existing order.[42]

South Africa in Barthian Perspective

Although various aspects of Barth's exegesis and interpretation of Romans 13:1-7 in his definitive exposition in "Church and State" have a bearing on the church-state question in South Africa today, I shall focus on three points in particular.

First, Barth correctly saw that if the New Testament is to be taken seriously in its understanding of the world, then the universal dominion it ascribes to Jesus Christ must include dominion over the ruling powers of this world, that is, they are part of the realm where Christ's Lordship is exercised, just as the church is a part of that realm. The New Testament claim is a bold one that often seems to be belied by reality, but the church, if it is to be a biblical one, must surely accept it and act on it. This is what gives legitimacy to Barth's theological attempt to co-opt the state for the kingdom of Christ. But it is also why the church cannot ignore the state as though the latter belonged to some other order of existence unrelated to the church. The evangelical and pietistic escapism of some segments of the church in South Africa from involvement with the state is certainly not biblically justified, particularly since this normally leads to an unquestioning support of the status quo.

Second, Barth rightly recognized that the church and the state as two forces within society inevitably encounter one another. The decisive question is whether their interests and activities conflict with one another or mutually support one another. Three basic possibilities would seem to exist:

1. The state may take a neutral or a positive stance regarding the church and its mission of proclaiming divine justification in Christ. This is the divinely intended relation of reciprocity in which the church, to use Barth's expression, guarantees the state through its prayers (1 Tim. 2:1-7) and through the respect its members have for the rulers of the state (Rom. 13:1-7). The state for its part guarantees the church's freedom by maintaining human justice (Rom. 13:1-7).

2. The state may refuse to tolerate the church and its mission; it may even attempt to suppress it. Whenever this occurs the state has defaulted if not repudiated its divinely ordained function in creating and administering human justice as laid down in Romans 13. Almost inevitably the suppression of the church goes hand-in-glove with the curtailment of true justice for other members of the society as well.

3. The third possibility, perhaps the most common in the contemporary world, is that the state may try to co-opt the church into supporting the ideology of the dominant group in the society. Civil religion, as it is called, is often insidious because the state appears to guarantee the freedom of the church. In return, however, it exacts a heavy price by circumscribing that freedom and by rendering the church unwilling or unable to speak on behalf of the poor and the oppressed for whom justice does not exist. It was the civil religion of the German Christians that, of course, gave rise to the Barmen Declaration, although it too failed to address the Jewish question adequately.[43] Suffice it to say, in terms of Barth's interpretation of the "demonic" state, when the state either suppresses or co-opts the church, then it has become "demonic."

In South Africa today, the ruling powers have attempted to suppress a segment of the church through intimidation. This is clear from the investigation of the recent Eloff Commission of Enquiry into the activities of the South African Council of Churches.[44] It is also apparent from the mass arrests of congregations involved in June 16 memorial services. Barth's work confirms that one of the marks of the unjust state is its attempt to tell the church what its business should and should not be and to force conformity to its will.[45] At the same time, the ruling group in South Africa, dominated by an ethnic minority, has also co-opted a segment of the church to support its ideology and its position of dominance within the society. By allowing itself to be co-opted, that part of the church has lost its prophetic role in society. Instead of criticizing the injustice and "demonic" character of the state and its apartheid ideology, the church has become a pillar in its maintenance.

Third, Barth has demonstrated that the church and its members can never offer absolute subjection to the state in terms of Romans 13:1-7. To be subject to a "demonic" state would mean a betrayal of the church's own nature. The church, Barth argued, must pray for the state, but this act in itself is a rejection of passive subjection. One cannot pray for the state without acting on that prayer. Thus if the state deviates from its divinely appointed role, then the church must recall it to its rightful task as God's agent for human justice. This means criticism of the state and even the acceptance of intimidation and persecution by the state. Certainly a segment of the church in South Africa has followed Barth's suggestions at this point. For Barth, however, this may not be enough. He goes so far as to argue that the church may have to contemplate rebellion against the state to "'overthrow with God' those rulers who do not follow the line laid down by Christ." There can be little doubt that Barth would have considered the possibility of such a radical action against a state that had the audacity to call itself Christian and then to perpetrate social injustice on a massive scale, to institutionalize oppresssion, to engage in terrorizing its own citizens in the name of law and order, and to attack its neighbors and support terrorism against them. For many Barth goes too far. Yet in 1938, he, unlike the politicians of his day, saw clearly that Hitler and Nazi Germany were "demonic" and could be stopped only by force.[46] Whether the churches of South Africa can or should go as far as Barth is a debatable point. What is not debatable is that all the churches owe their first and primary allegiance to Jesus Christ and through him to God. When God's demand for human justice is ignored or rejected by the state, then the church has no choice but to oppose the state and its rulers in order to call them back to their God-ordained task of ensuring human justice. The reason, Barth would say, is fundamentally theological. The church needs a just state if it is to carry out its primary task of preaching justification by faith.

Conclusions

Over the years Karl Barth's exegetical and interpretive style changed dramatically in keeping with his developing theological outlook. This led to the three very different expositions of Romans 13 and the church-state question in his writings. At an exegetical and interpretive level, there can be little doubt that Barth's changing method, for all its creativity and self-consistency, was largely idiosyncratic and therefore out of touch not only with the views of biblical scholars but also of many of his fellow theologians.[47] Nevertheless, Barth was in touch with the spirit of the writings of the New Testament in a way in which few theologians and perhaps even fewer biblical scholars have been in recent times. For this reason, his intepretation of Romans 13:1-7 and other New Testament texts concerned with the relation between the church and the state still have considerable relevance, particularly in a society like South Africa where the churches are viewed as significant forces both for and against social and political change. There can be no question, however, on which side of the ecclesiastical divide Barth would stand in this situation. The only issue is how radical would be his suggestion for the church at this time.

From Barmen to Belhar and Kairos

Nico Horn

Introduction

Comparing a recent confession with a historical one is a risky proposition. One can easily give in to the temptation of reading one's own
context into the works or confessions under discussion, forgetting the
historical background. Bearing in mind the possible, and even probable, misuse of confessions or theological works, it remains true that
older confessions can have significance for new situations. It is even
possible, as Cochrane has pointed out, that a confession, having arisen
in a particular setting, can lose its contextuality for a while, because
of a change of circumstances, and eventually achieve relevance again
in a new social setting. We find a good example of this in the *Düsseldorf Confession,* one of the early confessions of the German church
struggle, drawn up by Karl Barth and several other Reformed theologians in 1933. The Düsseldorf thesis begins with a repetition of the
first article of one of the oldest Reformed confessions, the Confession
of Berne (1528): "The holy Christian Church whose only Head is
Christ, is born of the Word, lives in it and hears not the voice of a
stranger."[1] No early confession could be more relevant for the Nazi
situation than this. At a time when the church was tempted to place its
hope in the Third Reich, Nazi ideology, and the person of Adolf
Hitler, Barth and his cosigners called the church, in the words of the
Berne fathers, to trust in Christ alone.

Much has been said about the similarities between the present
South African situation and the position of the church in Nazi Germany. Theologians such as Eberhard Bethge have warned against an
oversimplified identification of the two. That there are resemblances,

however, especially from a theological perspective, cannot be doubted.[2]

Karl Barth identified natural theology as the real heresy of the German Christians. The Jewish question in the church, the authoritarian powers of the Reich Bishop, and even the deification of the Third Reich were all symptoms of the "big sickness" of the German church.[3]

In South Africa the theology of apartheid and the state ideology of total separation arose in a completely different background. The underlying force of the development, however, was undoubtedly a natural theology, making the *volk* an order of creation and a source of revelation apart from and outside of Christ Jesus. This has been demonstrated by Douglas Bax, among others, in his evaluation of the Dutch Reformed paper, *Ras, Volk en Nasie*.[4]

Even in the political situations of Nazi Germany and contemporary South Africa there are more than just coincidental similarities. One would have to be very naive not to notice the influence of Nazi ideology on the early ideologists of apartheid. Professor Geoff Cronjé, who helped to lay the foundations for the apartheid ideology at the People's Congress in 1944, published in the same year a book in which he identified the Afrikaner as a superior race, a superiority seated in the blood, and spoke about the Jews as a separate race.[5]

We can expect, therefore, that the South African and German experiences would show certain similarities, in that both were built on more or less the same heresy. The continuous searching for pureness of blood, the idea of a *Herrenvolk,* the incrimination of "lower" races, discrimination against them—all result from a theological heresy that recognizes a source of revelation outside Christ (the history of the people) and from allowing so-called orders of creation to speak a more final word than God's Word in Jesus Christ. Even in political life we find certain recognizable similarities. The totalitarian trend of the Nationalist government, although not nearly as complete as that of the Third Reich, places it on common ground with the Nazis. In this essay I will evaluate the relevance of the Barmen Declaration to the political questions of the Third Reich and then compare it with the Draft Confession of the Nederduitse Gereformeerde Sendingkerk, concluding the discussion with passing reference to the Kairos Document.

The Barmen Declaration

The Barmen Declaration has its *Sitz im Leben* in the German church struggle. Although it is the best-known confessional document of its time, this declaration of the Confessing Church was not the only confessional document produced by the German church in that period. Cochrane identifies at least eight documents with a confessional character that preceded Barmen.[6]

Article 1

In the first article Jesus Christ, as attested in Scripture, is confessed as the One Word of God that we should hear, trust, and obey in life and death. It rejects the false doctrine that the church should recognize other events, powers, forms, and truths besides God's revelation.

Hans Asmussen points out that the heresy to which this article alludes is that of recognizing a second source of proclamation and revelation apart from Jesus Christ.[7] This was what happened in Germany when some Christians tried to force the National Socialist revolution on the church as a binding source of revelation. This was not, he adds, a matter of citizens protesting against the authority of the state. "For it is only a relative difference whether besides Holy Scripture in the Church, historical events or reason, culture, aesthetic feelings, progress of other powers and figures are said to be binding claims upon the Church."[8]

Eberhard Bethge sees the apolitical character of Barmen as its greatest shortfall. He points out that the real problems of German society—the Aryan paragraph, the neglect of human rights, excesses of law and order—are not addressed with the same fury as is the *falschen Altäre und Kanzelen*. According to him, this was why Bonhoeffer later turned to political conduct and moved away from the Confessing Church. Bethge also points out that the *status confessionis* moved from concern with the politically relevant Aryan paragraph in 1933 to the heresies of the *Glaubensbewegung* in the first months of 1934 and eventually to the malpractices of the church government.[9]

We need to bear in mind, however, that not everyone shares Bethge's evaluation of Bonhoeffer's discontent. Lovin points out that it was the Confessing Church's oath of loyalty to Hitler that made it imperative for Bonhoeffer to part in 1938.[10] G. Leibholz, who was not a theologian but was very close to Bonhoeffer, is of the opinion that Bonhoeffer's opposition to Hitler derived from the Barmen Declaration.[11] That is, Bonhoeffer's discontent was not with Barmen but with the Confessing Church, which had departed from the Barmen Declaration.

It is true that the first article of the declaration could have been more contextual. The heresy of the German Christians had, as Asmussen stated, definite political overtones. This, however, does not mean that the first Barmen article had no political relevance. Looking back at Barmen in his *Church Dogmatics,* Barth pointed out in 1940 that natural theology acquired a very specific content in Nazi Germany,

> namely the demand to recognize in the political events of the year 1933 and especially in the form of the "God-sent" Adolf Hitler, a source of specific new revelation of God, which, demanding obedience and trust, took its place beside the revelation attested in Holy Scripture, claiming that it should be acknowledged by Christian proclamation and theology as equally binding and obligatory.[12]

He also realized that once the state accepts, proclaims, or enforces a heresy, something which tends to happen, the church struggle takes on very evident political undertones. Although the Christian is still struggling against natural theology, the struggle becomes relevant for almost every political decision, chiefly because the state has lost its neutrality, or, as Barth puts it: "According to the dynamic of the political movement, what was already intended, although only obscurely outlined, in 1933, was the proclamation of this revelation as the only revelation, and therefore the transformation of the Christian Church into the temple of the German nature and history-myth."[13]

Article 2

This second article probably has a stronger political relevance than any other. It confesses Jesus Christ as God's assurance of the forgiveness of all sin, and that he is God's mighty claim upon our whole life. It also rejects the false doctrine that certain areas of our life do not belong to Jesus but to other gods and do not need justification and sanctification through him.

Cochrane points out that this article makes it very clear that *politics* is not an area exempt from the Lordship of Jesus Christ, and he adds, "The false doctrine of the separation of the two kingdoms, the spiritual and the temporal, was tacitly rejected."[14]

Johannes Hamel sees faithfulness to this article exemplified in the preaching of Martin Niemöller, which led to his arrest, in Barth's call on the churches of democratic Europe to support their governments in the struggle against "the beast from the abyss," and in the prayer liturgy of the Confessing Church in which the German church is called to confess its guilt and complicity in the threatening war.[15]

Walter Kreck points out that this article is a confession of the supreme rule of Christ. In this way the Barmen Declaration criticized the

Lutheran doctrine of the two kingdoms.[16] If Jesus Christ is God's mighty claim upon our whole life, the church cannot escape its duty to challenge the deeds of the state.

All this does not mean that the second Barmen article resolved the differences between church and state. Neither Barth nor the Confessing Church intended this. Even in 1938, after he had already moved into a much more political role against the Nazis, Barth did not ask for a just and Christian state, but only for a just state.[17] He stated specifically that "state as state knows nothing of the Spirit, nothing of love, nothing of forgiveness."

In his explanation of this article, Hans Asmussen notes that the church is not addressing the world, because the latter is not the church. "Consequently we would speak and we would have to speak in another tone if we were speaking to a world that attaches no value to being the church."[18] The roots and nature of the church make it possible for a synod to call the unfaithful to repentance with direct reference to the Lordship of Christ. The synod, however, cannot speak in the same tone to the state.

When the church finds itself in a totalitarian situation, its confession always has political and economical implications. The church does not confess against Hitler, but confesses the Lordship of Christ and renounces the heresy of the German Christians. When the state moves to intrude its political sovereignty upon religion, or when it demands total submission, this confession becomes socially, politically, and even economically important. An interesting example of the significance of this is Paul Schneider, who died in Buchenwald. He was beaten to death by SS guards when he refused to raise his hat to a Nazi flag. Under normal circumstances there would be nothing wrong in saluting a national flag. However, in a concentration camp where he already had been deprived of all his rights without a trial because of his faith, the lifting of a hat could mean acknowledging the Nazi totalitarian claims, which was utterly unacceptable.

Barth himself experienced the effects of this article when he was ordered by the rector of the University of Bonn to begin his lectures with the Nazi salute and when he was expected to take a personal oath of loyalty to the Führer. In both cases he refused because he saw it as an infringement of Christ's almighty claim upon our entire existence.

Article 3

In this article the church is confessed as the congregation of brothers and sisters in which Jesus Christ acts as Lord of the present, in Word and sacrament through the Holy Spirit. With its faith, obedience, message, and order the church community stands in the midst of the sinful world as pardoned sinners to testify that they are solely God's property and that they live and want to live solely in obedience to him and in the expectation of his return. Thus, it rejects the false doctrine that the church can alter its message and orders to suit prevailing ideologies or political convictions.

Many critics have stated that Barmen neglected the most crucial issue of the German society, the Aryan paragraph. Barth himself later felt he should have made the Jewish issue a decisive part of the confession.[19] Although the Aryan paragraph is not specifically mentioned, it is impossible to confess the church as the congregation of pardoned sinners and still make race or blood a prerequisite for church membership or office bearing in the church.

If one bears in mind that Article Two of the Rengsdorf Declaration, a confession made by prominent German Christians, stated that there was no such thing as universal Christianity and that Christianity as such is an abstraction, the link between Article 3 and the church becomes clear. That is, Article 3 of Barmen opposed an ideology that threatened to break down the barriers between church and state in order to make the church a dependent arm of the state. Where the first and second articles resist the concept of a sacralized state, Article 3 argues against the church becoming the state.

According to Hans Asmussen, "This message and . . . existence are rendered impossible for the church, however, the moment the boundary between the church and the world is blurred."[20]

Article 4

Article 4 is a clerical confession, but it is not without political relevance. This article is directed against the so-called *Reibi* or Reich Bishop. It states that the ministries or offices in the church are not based on the fixed dominion of some over others but exist for the ministry entrusted to and enjoyed by the whole congregation. Thus the article rejects the notion that the church needs a Führer with authoritarian power.

In *Theologische Existenz Heute* Barth had already observed that the agitation for a bishop was not vested in a real, existing need in the church but involved an imitation of the Führer concept.[21]

This article provides a good example of the connection between a word for the church, *Wort zur Sache,* and the church's word for the situation, *Wort zur Lage.* Helmut Gollwitzer has declared that Barth did not react against the *Lage* as such, but against the theologizing of the German Christians in the changing *Lage*. The German Christians, he says, deified the situation in Germany by omitting to ask what the consequences of the gospel in the changing situation ought to be.[22] While Barth was interested in the dialectical connection between the *Sache* and the *Lage,* German Christians misused the *Sache* to legitimate their preconceived political ideas.[23]

Brinkman notes that even in the period of *Theologische Existenz Heute* and Barmen, Barth's theology was never separate from his politics. In his battle with the German Christians and other *bindestrich-theologies,* however, it would have been hypocritical to encourage the church to become active in political opposition.[24]

Article 5

This article deals with the crucial relationship between church and state. With reference to 2 Peter 2:17 ("Fear God, honor Caesar"), Article 5 declares the state as an ordinance of God, according to Scripture, in the unredeemed world, with the task of providing justice and peace by means of order and the exercise of force. It rejects the false doctrine that the state can become a totalitarian force fulfilling the church's vocation as well, or that the church could and should appropriate the characteristic task and dignity of the state.

This article is not the doctrine of the two kingdoms "in disguise." It clearly rejects the possibility of the state becoming a totalitarian force. Although Asmussen observes that the article was directed against fallacies of the German Christians, it kept the possibility open that the church may indeed direct itself to the state.

> When the state proclaims an eternal kingdom, eternal righteousness, it corrupts itself and with it, its people. When the Church preaches a political kingdom, an earthly law, and the justice of a human form of society, it goes beyond its limits and drags the state down into the mire with it.[25]

The church and the state are not two completely alien kingdoms with nothing to say to each other. The church, however, cannot expect the state to be an alternative church or a Christian state. But it can call on the state to be a *Rechtstaat* or just state.

Cochrane argues that this article should have been interpreted more politically. Then the church would have had a more open mind for the fate of the Jews.[26]

Article 6

Article 6 declares that the mission of the church is to proclaim the message of God's grace in Jesus Christ to all people. This article also refers indirectly to the Jewish people. If God's grace must be proclaimed to all people, this includes the Jews. It is also, like articles 4 and 5, a corrective to those German Christians who appropriated the church and its message for the advancement of the German people alone.

Cochrane reminds us of Barth's words in the middle of World War Two: "What after all do we know about Adolf Hitler except that Jesus Christ died for him and that the book of life is not yet closed for him?"[27]

Although it is true that Barmen could have been more explicit in rejecting the heresies of its time, especially regarding the Jewish question, Barmen had definite political implications. I submit that we should see Barmen as falling within the church's traditional dealings with heresy. Since Nicea, confessions have always spoken against heresies, but with implications for other spheres of life.

This does not mean that the church cannot address the state. In 1936 the Confessing Church forwarded a memorandum to Hitler in which it warned against "positive Christianity" and the destruction of the church system. This was not a confession in itself, but a witness because of the existing confession. The Confessing Church did not blame the state for failing to bow before the Lordship of Christ, but only for preventing the Christian from bowing before Christ because of false indoctrination.

A prototype for Barmen (especially Article 2) can be found in the early church's confession, "Jesus is Lord." It is a christological confession of Christ's Lordship over one's whole life. Caesar is not mentioned, but the confession bears political implications for every Christian. If Jesus is Lord, Caesar cannot be such, and whatever the ruler claims, the Christian owes a greater allegiance to Christ. The Barmen Declaration rejects the heresy of the German Christians. Whenever the state accepts the pretensions of the false church, it brings the Christian into conflict with the state.

The Draft Confession of the N.G. Sendingkerk

Throughout the church's struggle against apartheid, the similarities between South Africa and Nazi Germany have been pointed out. We find examples of this as far back as July 1965, when Beyers Naudé wrote an article in *Pro Veritate* entitled "Die Tyd vir 'n Belydende Kerk is Daar" (It is Time for a Confessing Church).[28] However, in 1973 while visiting South Africa, Eberhard Bethge expressed the conviction that the term was not appropriate for the South African situation.

Since the late 1970s several churches have declared a *status confessionis* against apartheid. The Lutheran World Federation was the first mainstream church to do so. In August 1982 the World Alliance of Reformed Churches also declared a *status confessionis* against apartheid. At the same time the alliance accepted a paper on apartheid. In Article 11 of the paper the alliance declared, together with black Reformed Christians in South Africa, that apartheid (separate development) is sin, that its moral and theological justification makes a mockery of the gospel, and that such continuous unfaithfulness to the Word of God is heresy. In Article 8 the Alliance announced that it felt obligated to stand with the oppressed. Although the paper had definite political implications, it did not so much address a political ideology as a church in an intolerable political situation.

In September 1982 the Dutch Reformed Mission Church, meeting at synod, also declared a *status confessionis* against apartheid. It too accepted a paper of a commission that declared: "Because the secular gospel of apartheid threatens the confession of reconciliation in Jesus Christ and the unity of the Church of Jesus Christ in its foundation, the N. G. Mission Church declares that it creates a *status confessionis* for the church of Jesus Christ."

The paper also affirmed the Alliance's repudiation of apartheid and any moral and theological justification of it. The decision of the synod, however, differentiated between apartheid, which it called sin, and the theological justification of apartheid, which it called heresy.

After the acceptance of the *status confessionis,* Professor Gustav Bam, referring to Karl Barth, asked the synod to accompany it with a confession in which it rejected the false doctrine of apartheid. From his speech it would appear that he, together with those supporting the theological justification for the *status confessionis,* saw both the theology of apartheid and the political system itself as objects of the *status confessionis:* "I have come to a place where I understand and experience the apartheid system and its effects on my life, both from the state and the church, as contradicting the gospel of Jesus Christ as I understand it."[29]

This theological conviction, however, was not shared by everyone at the synod. Two of the signatories of the Draft Confession, professors Cloete and Smit, made a very clear distinction between the way the church speaks to the state and the way it addresses itself as church.[30] Smit rejected the idea that a political system can be a confessional question. "In ethical questions, that include political and ethical questions, the church usually has other forms of decision making, speech and conduct," and he pointed out that it can be "confusing and dangerously misleading to talk casually of a government which has betrayed and given up its God-given right to rule."[31] According to Smit, "the Mission Church was not to be caught in the trap of making a confession against a political system."[32] In his view, the Mission Church was protesting against an all-embracing ideology "that has historically and even presently, consciously or unconsciously, been affirmed, motivated and popularised from the Word. Against this the church confesses."

It is clear that Cloete and Smit stood much closer to Barmen than the other interpretations presented to the synod. In South Africa the political implications are especially striking because of the fact that apartheid as a political system was the offspring of heresy. It can with reasonable certainty be said that apartheid is even linked more closely to the theology of the Afrikaans-speaking churches than was the case in Nazi Germany.

If a confession of the Lordship of Jesus Christ in Germany meant civil disobedience for Barth in cases where the ungodly laws of the Nazis demanded totalitarian loyalty, surely the declaration of a *status confessionis* cannot mean anything less.

It seems clear that Smit and Cloete stood close to the spirit of the Draft Confession itself. The synod also accepted an Accompanying Letter, which further expressed the spirit of the Draft Confession. This letter expresses the spirit of Barmen, the church's answer to heresy. It emphasizes the seriousness of a confession—one can confess only if "the heart of the gospel is at stake." The focus is therefore on heresy in the *church,* especially in the Dutch Reformed churches; when the state is mentioned, it is in a different emphasis. The point of the letter is that the church allowed its heresy to influence the political system to the extent that the state became sacralized in a negative way. This is closely connected to Article 5 of Barmen, which rejected the heresy that the church should appropriate the characteristics, task, and dignity of the state.

The confession itself is much more explicit than Barmen and addresses the specific problems of South Africa much more openly than Barmen's implicit references to the Jewish question.[33]

The Draft Confession has more than one explicit connection with

Barmen. Like Barmen, it begins by confessing God; it differs, however, in that it confesses the triune God "who collects, defends and cares for his Church by His Word and Spirit." Thus, it notes the heresy of those South African churches who claimed the church for their political and ethnic groups alone. Like Barmen, the Draft Confession makes it clear that the church is the property of God who rules it by his Word and Spirit.

This very simple church confession, while not overtly political, carries tremendous political implications. It is common knowledge that the South African church often allowed specific racial groups to determine church policy. The Nationalist government has often been accused of dictating the directions of the church through the Broederbond. Abraham Lückhoff, in his doctoral thesis on Cottesloe, notes that at that time the Dutch Reformed Church delegation agreed with several positive views on the racial situation. After the intervention of Prime Minister Verwoerd, however, the church made a roundabout turn, purely politically inspired, and those delegates who persisted in their original views were discredited.[34]

The second article of the Draft Confession is more contextual and explicit than any of the articles of the Barmen Declaration. It deals with what is perhaps the most relevant theological question within the Dutch Reformed Church family—the unity of the church. Like Barmen, this article begins with the confession of a doctrinal truth. It repeats Article 8 of the *Apostolicum,* adding the words "called from the entire human family." To state belief in "one holy universal Christian Church, the communion of saints," has always been meant to imply that no political apartheid structure can exist in the church. This old biblical truth has been so weakened by ideology, however, that it has become necessary to make an addition to make it clear that the church consists of *all* God's called people, irrespective of any other consideration, such as race.

In the next paragraph Christ's work of reconciliation is confessed as being manifested in the church in the community of believers who have been reconciled with God and with one another.

Although this section deals primarily with the unity of the church, as based on the second and third articles of the Christian faith, it is not without political relevance. The reason why Christians refuse to drink of the same cup, and why race should be a condition for membership of the church, is because the church has accepted a worldview alien to the gospel. To accept the Draft Confession's rejection of this worldview in the church inevitably leads to a rejection of any political system with a similar worldview. Therefore one cannot agree with

Strauss that this article divides the world and church into two king-doms and that it is just another form of church-centeredness in that it speaks only of the unity in Christ in the church and not in society.[35]

In the third paragraph the state is brought directly into the picture. "The credibility of this message is seriously affected . . . in a land which professes to be Christian, but in which enforced separation of people on a racial basis promotes and perpetuates alienation, hatred and enmity." The words "which professes to be Christian" are the heart of the confession. The church does not call for a Christian state, but confesses against an ideology that claims to be the gospel.

Paragraph 4 states clearly that this forced separation is sin and any teaching that attempts to legitimate it by an appeal to the gospel must be considered false doctrine. The rejection that follows Article 3 clearly repudiates any doctrine that would sanction separation "and thereby in advance . . . weaken the ministry and experience of recon-ciliation in Christ."

The protest in Article 3 does not oppose a political system but rather a false gospel. It does, however, express very clearly the fact that the policy of apartheid is immoral. The aim of the confession, like Barmen, is to state the church's position; only in a secondary manner, through its witness as "salt of the earth," is it to critique the immoral-ity of society.

Article 4 of the confession deals with justice. God is confessed as the "One who wishes to bring about justice and true peace among men" and "in a special way the God of the destitute, the poor and the wronged." The church as God's possession is called to stand where he stands against injustice and with the wronged and to confront the powerful and privileged who would selfishly seek only their own in-terests and thus control and harm others.

Smit points out that this confession is of great importance be-cause blacks experience apartheid as unjust, humiliating, and oppres-sive. Therefore "moral or theological justification of the separation theology [is] fully an attempt to defend an unjust society as Biblical or Christian."[36] The Draft Confession does not combat natural the-ology in the same way as Barmen did, but it repudiates the results of the Afrikaner churches' own natural theology (the theology of apart-heid) even more effectively.

De Gruchy has pointed out that whereas there were no Jews pres-ent at Barmen,[37] Belhar is a product of the oppressed themselves. This is probably the reason why Belhar would serve as a corrective to Bar-men's silence on the Jewish question.

The Kairos Document

Although some *status quo* theologians in South Africa have claimed that the Kairos Document is "untheological," there are striking similarities between it and the writings of the young Barth, especially one of Barth's first papers, "Jesus Christ and the Movement for Social Justice," read to the labor movement in Safenwil in 1911.[38]

In this article, Barth claimed a very strong association between the movement for social justice and the commands of Jesus Christ, while simultaneously rejecting the possibility of making the same connection between Christ and the church. "Jesus is the movement for social justice and the movement for social justice is Jesus." Again: "The church is not Jesus and Jesus is not the church."

The accusation that the Kairos Document sees people only as part of a structure and not as individuals could also be made of Barth. Not only does he describe the movement for social justice as the real content of the person of Jesus, he sees it as "a direct continuation of the spiritual power which . . . entered into history and life with Jesus."[39] He also interprets socialism as the way of salvation.

> If you understand the connection between the person of Jesus Christ and your socialist convictions, and if you now want to arrange your life so that it corresponds to this connection, then that does not mean you have to believe this, that or the other thing. What Jesus has to bring to us are not ideas, but a way of life. Man can have Christian ideas about God and the world or about man and redemption, and still with all that be a complete heathen. And as an atheist, a materialist, and a Darwinist, one can be a genuine follower of and disciple of Jesus."[40]

To a certain extent the connection between Jesus and socialism is even stronger. The Kairos Document nowhere states that Jesus Christ *is* the socialist movement, only that he takes up the cause of the poor and oppressed and identifies himself with their interests.

There are, however, certain differences. Whereas the Kairos Document takes up the cause for the oppressed somewhat uncritically, Barth makes it clear that his identification is with the cause of socialism and not with the praxis of some or even all of the Social Democrats.[41] Only in this way is Jesus a real socialist. Barth also criticizes the praxis of the movement. He would not allow any one group, not even the socialists, to "capture" Jesus for themselves. Should anyone conclude from his speech that Barth himself thought the socialists were right, Barth stated explicitly, "I have spoken about what the socialists want, not the manner in which they act to attain it. But I fail to see what good such acts would accomplish." He went on:

Your concerns are in line with the concerns of Jesus. Real socialism is real Christianity in our time. That may fill you with pride and satisfaction about your concerns. But I hope you have also heard the rebuke implied in the disfunctions I have made between Jesus and yourselves. . . . Leave the superficiality and the hatred, the spirit of Mammon and the self-seeking, which also exist among your ranks, behind.[42]

Even the accusation of Marxist influence can be made applicable to Barth himself. Barth sees an analogy of the Bible's identification with the oppressed in the solidarity of workers as expressed in the words of the *Communist Manifesto* of 1848: "Proletarians of the world unite!"

It is, however, my intention here to compare the Kairos Document with Barmen and not with the young Barth. Marquardt and Gollwitzer, among others, have suggested that the sentiments of the early Barth were actually the Magna Carta of his whole theology. Reading Barth from this perspective, it would be possible to come to quite different conclusions about the real meaning of Barmen, as Gollwitzer has indeed done.[43] Such an interpretation would bring Barmen much closer to the popular interpretation of the Draft Confession and to the Kairos Document.

The Kairos Document does not present itself as a confession but as "a Christian, biblical and theological comment on the political crisis in South Africa today." This is probably the clearest distinction between Barmen and the Draft Confession on the one hand and the Kairos Document on the other. The crisis to which the document refers is summarized in one paragraph in the first section: "In the life and death conflict between different social groups that has come to a head in South Africa today, there are Christians (or at least people who profess to be Christians) on both sides of the conflict—and some who are trying to sit on the fence." The document then identifies these three approaches as *State Theology* (those who support the *status quo*), *Church Theology* (those who sit on the fence—the so-called English-speaking churches), and *Prophetic Theology,* the theology advocated by the document.

Possibly the most significant theological difference between Barmen and the Kairos Document is the fact that Barmen is a christological document, denying natural theology a right of existence in the church, whereas the Kairos Document maintains that the "first task of a prophetic theology for our times would be an attempt at social analysis or what Jesus would call 'reading the signs of the time' (Mt. 16:3) or 'interpreting this Kairos' (Lk. 12:56)."

The Kairos Document analyzes the social setting in South Africa and then gives biblical answers to contemporary social questions. In its critique of "Church Theology," the document sees the lack of a developed social analysis as the fundamental problem of this kind of theology. "As we all know, spirituality has tended to be an otherworldly affair that has little, if anything at all, to do with the affairs of the world." This as we have seen, is not the case with either Barmen or Belhar.

If we see the Kairos Document as an open document, "a basis for further discussion by all Christians in the country," the theological differences between it and the Barmen Declaration need not be emphasized. Unlike Barmen and Belhar, the Kairos Document does not claim to speak a final word on the heresies in the church, but to be a landmark on the way.

It is not only possible but also probable that as the Kairos Document leads to further discussion it will strengthen the confessional movement in South Africa. The similarity between the Kairos Document and Barmen lies in the fact that both addressed a crucial issue at a crucial stage. Despite theological differences, the Kairos Document, like Barmen and Belhar, protests against a church caught up in false ideology.

No matter how much one's own theology differs from that of the Kairos Document, one cannot ignore the cry of protest and urgency in it. Neither can one deny the existence of the unjust state with its supposed "theology" that the Kairos Document seeks to address. In this sense the document can be seen as a call for repentance. We can only hope that this call will urge Christians in South Africa once again to take the confessional movement seriously.

The example of Karl Barth has played an important role in the confessional movement in South Africa. Not only did he popularize the term *status confessionis,* but his theology, especially the Barmen Declaration, clearly influenced the Draft Confession of the Mission Church and other confessional writings. Perhaps the young Barth's relationship with the socialists of his time can serve as an example for Christians in their response to the Kairos Document. Although Barth did not approve of all their deeds, nor of all their teachings, he gave them critical support because he shared their ideals. Barth heard the cry of the exploited workers of his time and stood alongside them, because, according to him, that was where Jesus stood.

Church and State in South Africa: Karl Barth vs. Abraham Kuyper

Jaap Durand

Central to the debate on the apartheid system in South Africa is the question of the role of the church, not only in its relationship to the state, which enforces the system by legal and other means, but also as far as the development of the ideological basis of apartheid itself is concerned. In both instances the focus falls on the Dutch Reformed churches, for it has been clearly pointed out and accepted by historians that these churches played a vital part in giving to apartheid a theological basis[1] and, because of that, uncritically supporting the Nationalist government's implementation of apartheid measures.

The fact that apartheid is not merely a political policy, but an ideology and a system of beliefs that involves both state and church, almost inevitably begs a comparison between the South African situation and the conditions that prevailed in Germany under the Nazi regime. A lot has been said, and justifiably so, about the impropriety of equating the South African situation with Nazi Germany of the 1930s, but the fact remains that there is a basic similarity between the two situations, insofar as we have in both instances to do with a state ideology more or less supported by the official church and sanctioned by a kind of natural theology that takes creation and the so-called "orders of creation" as its point of departure. It is no wonder that comparisons are made between the theological situation during the years when an apartheid theology was being worked out and the theological developments at the time of the German church struggle under the Nazi regime. It is almost inevitable that the name of Karl Barth should crop up here and questions be asked about the possible effect his thought may have had on resistance to this development of Afrikaner theology, in that his theological approach with its emphasis on the centrality of Christ and his crusade against all forms of natural theology formed the immediate springboard for the Barmen Declaration, which openly heralded the beginning of the struggle against Nazi ideology in the German churches.

Unfortunately, Barth's theological influence in this area was negative as far as the three most crucial decades in the development of Afrikaner Reformed theology are concerned. During this period, from the beginning of the 1930s to the end of the 1950s, Barthian theology had such a formidable opponent in Kuyperianism that it was never able to obtain a firm foothold in the field of Afrikaner theological thinking. The reasons for this are not too difficult to find.

First, Barth's theology was regarded as suspect because his views on Scripture did not conform to the orthodox Reformed standpoint generally accepted in South Africa during those years. No one seemed to realize that Barth's theoretical view on the authority and inspiration of Scripture very seldom, if ever, materially affected his use of Scripture. The way in which Barth himself used Scripture in his *Church Dogmatics* was just as "orthodox" as any usage by Kuyperians, but the fear that Barthian theology might undermine the authority of Scripture could not be allayed. Second, and more important, the Afrikaner version of Kuyperian theology was much more subtle and less crude in its cosmological approach than the German *Ordnungstheologie*. Moreover, Kuyperian cosmology was combined with orthodox Reformed Christology in such a way that any attempt to subject theology to christological criticism, as was done in Germany, would have been frustrated from the outset. The dormant natural theology in the Afrikaner version of Kuyperianism was therefore never recognized for what it was. As a result, Barth's criticism of religion and of natural theology was never really heard in those Kuyperian circles that needed it most during the formative years of Afrikaner Reformed theology.[2] It was only as late as the 1960s, and particularly in the early 1970s, that the Barthian resistance to a creation theology began to take hold among young Afrikaner theologians and new thoughts with a definite Barthian flavor made significant inroads into the debate on church and society.

The introduction of Barthian theology and the revolution of the church-state relationship within Dutch Reformed circles did not, however, serve to clarify this debate. On the contrary, greater confusion resulted because the Barthian model for church-state relationships challenged the seemingly clear understanding of this relationship in Kuyperian theology. During the same period a further development in theology compounded the problem. A new awareness of the hermeneutical problems involved in interpreting a text within a given situation came to the fore—in this case the question of whether theologians drawing on the Bible can make meaningful pronouncements about any subject, given the historical gap between biblical times and the present. Any attempt to compare and evaluate the respective influences of Barthian and Kuyperian theology on the issue of the relationship between state and church in South Africa must therefore take this hermeneutical problem into consideration. In this essay I shall accordingly try to address the hermeneutical problem and thus establish the comparative effectiveness of the two Reformed models under consideration with respect to the church's prophetic calling vis-à-vis state and society. But to do this, the hermeneutical problem must first be more clearly defined and the two models explained, each within its own theological framework. Once this is done a clearer understanding will follow of how these models have influenced South African society and continue to exert influence today.

Defining the Problem

The problem of the relationship between church and state is not new. It has accompanied the church for almost twenty centuries without being resolved. Answers given in certain times and situations prove inadequate when circumstances change and new issues appear. The roots of this struggle for theological clarity may be traced to the Bible itself, in that the Bible does not provide a detailed and complete treatise on this difficult subject. The Bible, as God's authoritative witness to his revelation in history, treats problems such as these in a historical way. Scriptural normativity is so closely interwoven with the historical context that a direct application of what are sometimes called "biblical principles" can often be a hazardous and even misleading undertaking. For example, *prima facie* we have in Romans 13 a clear-cut directive to which the apostle Paul addresses himself. We discover the same in 1 Peter 2:11-17. It seems as if in both cases we are presented with a quiet and well-ordered society in which the relationship between the state and its Christian citizens is clearly defined. But Revelation 13 portrays the state in its diabolical rebellion against God and its persecution of the church. The whole passage vibrates with this tension. This discrepancy between different approaches in the Bible arises from the different historical contexts in which they were written; and for this reason a straightforward, literal application of any of these approaches to present-day circumstances can be deceptive.

If we were to look for any direct pronouncement in the Bible about the role of the church toward the state, apart from the exhortation to be submissive in all things that do not contradict the revealed will of God, we should look in vain. This qualification is important, but aside from it, the call to submission is the essence of church-state relations in the New Testament.

The Old Testament is not helpful either, because we cannot impose here our ideas of what church and state ought to be. Church and state were too undifferentiated in those times for the Old Testament to be useful or exemplary for us. The normativity should be sought on a different level. Whoever therefore looks for direct scriptural data on the prophetic task of the church vis-à-vis the state will be greatly disappointed. It is not direct scriptural evidence but rather the particular theological system and even the general theological approach that determine the outcome of our reflection on church-state relations.

Our basic understanding of the way of salvation, and consequently our understanding of what the church is, have direct consequences for our view of the functions of the church in society and its responsibility toward the powers that be. The two mainstream traditions of Christian faith in the West, Roman Catholic and Protestant, bear witness to this fact.

In Roman Catholicism the main theological emphasis falls on the sacrament as the vehicle of salvation. The church is seen as the bearer of the sacrament; thus, by virtue of its authority to administer the sacraments, the church is the mediator of salvation. On the basis of the well-known adage, *gratia non tollit naturam, sed perficit,* the church is called to bring all the natural spheres of life, including the state, to a higher level of perfection. This can be achieved only by church control and guardianship over these natural spheres. Control rather than prophetic witness was therefore the watchword of the Roman Catholic Church after the Council of Trent. Since Vatican II the emphasis has shifted from the idea of control and guardianship to that of the mutual penetration *(compenetratio)* of church and world.[3]

Within Protestantism salvation is not defined in terms of the sacraments. Rather, with emphasis on the living Word of God, the church is seen in the first place as bearer of the Word. However, not all the different groups within Protestantism will conclude from this fact that the church has a prophetic task vis-à-vis the state. In the Lutheran idea of the two kingdoms, and in particular in the nineteenth-century affirmation of it, we find a Protestant tradition that emphasizes the distinctiveness of the two spheres of church and state to such a degree that the possibility for the prophetic voice of the church to lose its significance becomes very strong.[4] On the basis of a dialectical tension between law and gospel in Lutheran thought, the worldly regiment of the state makes use of the law and the sword, whereas in the spiritual regiment of the church the gospel reigns. The demands of the gospel cannot be applied to the state. In effect this too often has resulted in the silence of the church over against the state, which may not be what Luther himself intended.

Within the Reformed tradition we find a different approach. Like Luther, Calvin distinguished between a civil and a spiritual regiment, but at the same time he differed from Luther by stressing the inner coherence of the two regiments. This coherence corresponds with the coherence between law and gospel in Calvin's thought, and consequently with the characteristic Reformed belief in the sovereignty of the law of God over life in its totality. In this context the Word of God exercises an all-embracing function.[5]

Through the Word the spiritual regiment should bring the worldly regiment into submission to the reign of Christ in a manner more decisive than in Luther's case. This is Calvin's significant contribution to the very difficult problem of the two regiments. They are bound together by the sovereignty of Christ, but the first regiment, and therefore the church, retains priority; for in the church Christ reigns directly through Word and Spirit and only through the proclamation of this same Word does his reign extend to state and society. From this follows the conviction that the church as bearer of the Word has a prophetic task with regard to the state.

This sounds rather basic to those who accept and share the Reformed belief in the sovereignty of Christ in all spheres of life. There are, however, two basic problems that we need to deal with before speaking too glibly about the prophetic voice of the church in matters that affect state and society. The first problem is that within the Reformed tradition the inner coherence between the two regiments is never allowed to annihilate the distinctiveness of the two. Accordingly, both church and state as the embodying of the two regiments have their own functions and power, each within its own spheres. We must therefore ask the question: In what way should the prophetic voice of the church be heard in view of the sphere-sovereignty of the state?

The second problem is even more serious and concerns the way in which the church should proclaim the Word of God vis-à-vis the state, bearing in mind that the church cannot proclaim the Word without first having understood the Word of God for a concrete and specific situation. In other words, we are faced with the most difficult of all theological problems: the hermeneutical problem.

How, then, are we to understand the ethical norms of Scripture for a specific political situation? And in which way can the church confront the state with these norms without trespassing into the sphere of the state?

Because these two problems are not fundamental to the whole subject that we are dealing with and are also difficult to answer in themselves, we should not be surprised to find that in the history of the Reformed tradition different answers have been given and different systems developed, although all of them understood themselves as legitimate continuations from Calvin's original starting-point. We can distinguish between three basic Calvinistic models: the Kuyperian model, the Barthian model, and the model developed by Van Ruler.[6] Of these three, the models developed by Kuyper and Barth are not only more influential but also the only two that have had significant influence on the South African setting. We shall therefore examine these two models before attempting to relate them to the South African situation and to gauge their effect on the shaping of South African society with regard to the church-state relationship.

The Kuyperian Model

With Kuyper we are faced with a definite modification of Calvin's idea, although Kuyper wished to remain true to the original intentions of the great reformer.[7] It is well known that he made the statement that there is no part of life of which Christ does not say that it belongs to him. Less well known is the fact that Kuyper made only limited use of this idea in his views on the relation between church and state. In fact, he arrived at a model that showed remarkable similarities to the idea of the two kingdoms in Lutheran orthodoxy.[8] Directly responsible for this state of affairs was his understanding of the relationship of *common grace* and *particular grace*.

According to Kuyper, common grace finds its starting point in the fact that God sustains his original creation. Through common grace God wants to check the full development of sin, which, unhindered, would make life itself impossible. Thus common grace involves all humanity, believers as well as unbelievers. Its characteristic is to conserve rather than to renew. The state finds its origin in the area of common grace; the church, on the other hand, finds its origin in the particular grace of the Word and of regeneration.

In accordance with his distinction between common and particular grace, Kuyper differentiated between the power and authority of Christ as the mediator of creation (i.e., as the second Person of the Godhead) and the authority of Christ as mediator of our salvation. As mediator of our salvation, Christ is restricted to the sphere of the church as the only possible earthly form of organization for the kingdom of God. All other forms of organization in society, the state included, have to do with common grace and are therefore not subjected to the direct authority of Christ as the mediator of salvation. In the world outside the church Christ rules as the mediator of creation.[9]

Thus we have the spiritual rule of Christ as the head of his church and the king of God's kingdom alongside the rule of the worldly powers who receive their authority from the triune God and not from Christ. Any possibility for a Christian state as such is therefore excluded. Clearly Kuyper approaches the Lutheran idea of the two kingdoms in this respect rather than adhering to the original intent of Calvin. In the end, however, he does not become a "disciple of Luther," because he continues to support the Reformed conviction that sanctification embraces the whole life of the believer and is not restricted to the institutional life of the church or the religious life of the individual.

But how does sanctification come about? In what way does Christ exercise his spiritual authority in state and society? Kuyper answers this question by making use of two basic concepts: the principle of sphere-sovereignty and the distinction between the church as an institution and the church as an organism according to the principle of sphere-sovereignty. He argues that Christ's spiritual power is not exercised in state and society by means of the church as an institution or organization. Each sphere of human society has its own authority, derived from God, and its own function in accordance with the character of that particular sphere. The church as the organization of particular grace is one life-sphere among others. Accordingly it must respect the boundaries of the other spheres, including that of the state.

In effect this means that the church should confine itself to its own particular calling: the preaching of the Word of God and the administering of the sacraments. As soon as the church does more than this—for example, getting involved in practical politics, in which it prescribes courses of action to the state—it oversteps the boundaries of church and particular grace to violate the sphere-sovereignty of the state. However, according to Kuyper, the church is more than an institution; in fact, it is not primarily an institution at all. More than anything else, it is an organism consisting of the regenerated who move and live in all spheres of life. This is the true church that Kuyper even identifies with the invisible church. Living in all spheres of life, these reborn elect exercise their influence by means of Christian organizations. With respect to the state, this implies the formation of a Christian political party, by means of which the invisible church of true believers exercises influence. The institutional church has no direct function in this respect. In other words, the institution's influence on the life of the people, the society, and the state will always be indirect, via the church as an organism of believers. This implies, furthermore, that in Kuyper's view the prophetic calling of the church in political matters is not that of the church as institution, but as organism. This reduces to a minimum the possibility of tensions between church and state. The struggle to maintain Christian norms in the political sphere is to be waged by a Christian political party as the prophetic mouthpiece.

A fundamental difficulty arises from this concept. The distinction between the church as institution and the church as organism can lead to a division between the two, with so much emphasis on the organism that the institutional church as bearer of the Word of God is virtually silenced in matters that pertain to state and society.[10] Even though this was perhaps not Kuyper's original intent, the conclusion can be (and has been) drawn by some of his epigones, especially in South Africa. But I shall return to this problem after dealing with the model suggested by Karl Barth, who emphasizes the direct prophetic task of the institutional church far more than does Kuyper.

The Barthian Model

As with Kuyper, so with Karl Barth: a definite continuity exists between his ideas and Calvin's original starting point. In certain respects, however, Barth goes his own way, motivated by his outspoken wish to eradicate the last traces of the "doctrine of the two kingdoms" in the Reformed tradition. We may expect, then, that Barth would differ from Kuyper in some fundamental aspects.

Barth's view is supported by two main pillars of thought, both well grounded in his theology: the christological foundation of the state and the gospel-law relationship. According to Barth, the Reformers identified state and law too exclusively with the orders of creation and providence. As a result, they were unable to articulate in what way political power was grounded in the power and sovereignty of Christ. What Barth wishes to make clear here is that Calvin's view on the two regiments is not fully integrated with his belief in the kingship of Christ. This deficiency can be overcome, says Barth, only if the state is related to the center of the Christian belief—Christ, the crucified and risen Lord, the king of God's kingdom and of the kingdoms of the earth.

In his assessment of the state, Barth does not take the idea of creation and sin as his point of departure. Instead he starts from the decisive fact of Jesus Christ and his kingdom. He argues that the state is not a product of sin but belongs to the order of divine grace. In the state we do not come across a general Creator-god but the Father of Jesus Christ. Although the state is part of the human order with its own function and purpose, it is never autonomous: it has a place and a function within God's plan of salvation. In one of the most crucial meetings of all time, that between Jesus and Pilate, the earthly order of justice and the state has some definite connection with the order of salvation of the kingdom of God.

Barth bases this idea on his dogmatic supposition that the gospel precedes the law. If, according to his famous definition, the law is the *form* of the gospel with grace as its *content,* it is impossible to say that in the worldly realm of politics and the state the law reigns supreme while in the spiritual realm of the church the gospel rules. Rather, human existence in both realms is determined by the gospel. The state therefore cannot go its own way as if the salvation of humankind has not commenced in Christ.

In his *Christian Community and Civil Community,*[11] Barth uses the image of two concentric circles to explain his line of thought. The Christian congregation forms the inner, smaller circle, and the civil congregation the larger outer circle. The common hub of these two circles is Jesus Christ and the proclaimed kingdom of God. What, then, is the relationship between the two concentric circles and their common center, and between the two circles themselves? Barth's answer is that the light of God's kingdom falls on the church and from there is reflected onto the state. The relationships are *analogous* in character. By virtue of the common center, the state has the right of existence as a paradigm, as an analogy of the kingdom of God as proclaimed in the church. In this respect the political responsibility of the Christian community emerges. Through its existence and its preaching the church must remind the state of the kingdom of God, so that the state can become a mirror-image and paradigm of the kingdom. The true state finds in the true church its primordial example.

Barth gives a long list of examples to indicate how the exemplary existence of the church expresses itself. We can consider but a few. Because God became human, the Christian community is concerned about the fate of all humanity in the political arena and not about some abstract cause or other; because in Christ God established his justice among humankind, the Christian community will always advocate a just state, rejecting anarchy as well as tyranny; because the Son of Man came to save those who were lost, the Christian community sides with the weak and the poor while it strives for social justice.

The important question now is: In what way should the Christian congregation realize its exemplary life-style? The first answer is that the Christian will always choose that political possibility in which the analogy of belief and message takes form. The question has been asked whether or not Christians should establish a Christian political party. Barth rejects this, asking instead whether there can be any other Christian "party" in the state apart from the Christian community itself whose task embraces the totality of state and society. He argues that that which is Christian can never become directly visible "in the political sphere." It can only operate indirectly as a mirror-image and a paradigm. In practice it may well happen that the Christian message can become an embarrassment for a Christian political party if it is not able to find political room for that message. It is therefore possible that the Christian party may compromise the Christian community and its message. Therefore the Christian must always act anonymously in the political field.

The anonymity of Christians in the political sphere, however, is replaced by visibility in a church that speaks out. In the church the preaching inevitably becomes political and an aware congregation will understand the political implications even though nothing is said about politics. But the church does not speak only through its preaching of the good news. It is part of the church's duty to make its political decisions known by means of notification from the pulpit and by other official steps. In this respect the church should see to it that it does not awaken from its apolitical sleep only when state lotteries and the desecration of the Sabbath are at stake. More important is the necessity for the church to be truly the church. Within the state the church speaks the loudest through being what it is. In this sense the church is *ipso facto* a political factor.

The South African Situation and the Hermeneutical Problem

When we compare the Kuyperian and Barthian models, both of which claim continuity with Calvin, it becomes evident that whereas the

Kuyperian model combines an active Christian witness in the political field with an almost silent church, the Barthian model does the exact opposite: combines a prophetic church with politically silent Christians as *Christians*. Direct political action and witness is done anonymously.

In spite of this fundamental difference, both models have in common the fact that they tend to restrict the all-embracing outreach of the Word of God; rather, they make it ineffectual in one "part" of the church. If, for the sake of our argument, we wish to retain the Kuyperian distinction between the church as an institution and the church as an organism—although aware of the danger of making a distinction that Barth does not make and in so doing being unfair to him—we may express it as follows: Kuyper's model makes the prophetic political outreach of the Word of God ineffectual in the institutional church by burying it beneath generalities, while Barth's model, seeing the church as an organism, buries the Word of God in anonymity.

Such a comparison between Kuyper and Barth can be very misleading, however, if we think in terms of the consequences of their respective points of departure especially in relation to the South African setting. Because of the singular nature of the South African situation, the basic defect in the Kuyperian model had far more serious consequences than the Barthian model would have suffered had it been given the same opportunities to influence Afrikaner theological thought patterns. When the Barthian viewpoint eventually did appear on the South African scene, its corrective influence on the existing Kuyperian model outweighed any possible negative effects arising from the former's emphasis upon Christian anonymity in the social and political field. A closer look at the way in which Afrikaner Reformed thinking in fact used the Kuyperian model to make the Word of God ineffectual with respect to the state's policy of oppression will explain why.

We have already pointed out that Kuyper's distinction between the church as an institution and the church as an organism can lead to a situation in which the institutional church is silenced, because it has handed over its prophetic task to Christian organizations of the church as an organism. Where no such Christian organization exists, for instance in the political field, this means that the church has completely abandoned its prophetic calling for that specific sphere of life (unless, of course, the church as an institution takes over that role). This is precisely what happened in South Africa. Due to historical and other circumstances only one aspect of the Kuyperian model has been implemented in South Africa. The formation of a Christian political party was never realized. As a matter of fact the prime movers behind Kuyperianism in South Africa during the 1930s and 1940s never considered seriously the possibility of forming a Christian party in the Kuyperian sense. Whereas Kuyper himself most surely would have found such a partial implementation of his ideas completely unacceptable, his epigones in South Africa were perfectly content with their "adaptation."

There is a very good reason for this.[12] The Kuyperians in South Africa never considered the Nationalist Party un-Christian, or at any rate un-Christian enough to merit the establishment of a Christian political party. In their opinion, on the contrary, the Nationalist Party conformed in a broad sense to Christian values. Kuyperians, we must recall, were, together with the majority of Afrikaners, the victims of Afrikaner civil religion. They considered the Afrikaner people a nation called by God to christianize the heathen, to establish Christian civilization in Africa, and to preserve Western values. For them the Nationalist Party was the political embodiment of those ideals, just as the Afrikaner churches fulfilled the religious calling of the Afrikaner through missionary work among the black nations of southern Africa.

Furthermore, the second arm of the Kuyperian model, the respect of the church for the sphere-sovereignty of the state shown by not indulging in practical politics, suited them perfectly. The reason for this can also be located in the phenomenon of Afrikaner civil religion. Civil religion provides social cohesion and legitimates its systems by creating a communal purpose: in this instance the "calling" of the Afrikaner in Africa and the concomitant need for self-preservation against alien and hostile forces. It is clear that in these circumstances, the Afrikaner Reformed churches, far from criticizing the existing structures of South African society, supplied the religious motivation for condoning and even advocating a discriminatory and oppressive system for the sake of self-preservation and self-legitimation. In later years, when moral pressure from the ecumenical movement made it almost impossible to support and defend the apartheid system openly, these churches simply kept quiet for the sake of the unity and cohesion of the nation. Civil religion preserves the cohesion of society: there is no place in it for biblical prophets; for the message of a prophet divides and society cannot afford division in the face of threatening forces. So the most a church should be willing to do when its conscience is stirred would be to confront the government quietly and privately. The fewer who know about it, the better.

Of course the Afrikaner churches have never denied the prophetic responsibility of the Christian church vis-à-vis the state. Such a denial would have been too obvious a departure from the Reformed tradition. The Kuyperian model showed them a way out of this dilemma. Kuyperians argued more or less along these lines: although the church has a prophetic calling, it should proclaim only general Christian principles and refrain from any form of concretizing these principles for fear of impinging on the sphere-sovereignty of the state and indulging in party politics. Although this argument has a certain amount of validity, inasmuch as the church is certainly not a political party, the very real danger remains that the prophetic voice of the church in political matters will be buried beneath generalities. Precisely because general principles and not specifics are proclaimed the church forsakes its hermeneutical task of understanding and *interpreting* the Word of God for a given historical-political situation. The responsibility for such an interpretation is left to the individual Christian. That he or she should interpret the Word of God in the political field, or for that matter any other field in his or her own specific circumstances, is of course not wrong. On the contrary, such an idea is part and parcel of the Reformed tradition that has always emphasized the fact that the believer has direct access to the Bible without the mediating function of the church. It was never the intention of the Reformers, however, to eliminate the church and the ministry of the Word. The ministry of the Word is, *inter alia,* a safeguard against an individualistic and arbitrary interpretation of the Bible. The Word of God stresses the fact that we can know only "with all God's people" (Eph. 3:18), that is, within the community of the church. To maintain that the church should proclaim only "general Christian principles" or "eternal truths" without the necessary hermeneutical process of trying to understand what "general Christian principles" means in a specific historical situation is to undermine the ministry of the Word or to make it a caricature of what it should be.

This is what happened and is still happening to a great degree in the Afrikaner churches. It is not unusual to listen to lofty sermons about social justice within these circles, but very seldom is it spelled out what social justice entails for us in South Africa today. As soon as the church is asked to be more specific about certain issues, such as the Group Areas Act, the problem of political representation for the black people of South Africa, or the creation of nonviable "independent states," the questioner is told that the church is not called to participate in practical politics. That all these issues have a very definite moral aspect is completely ignored. The end result is that the church is reduced to silence, and by its very silence endorses things that cannot be tolerated on moral grounds and in the light of the gospel.

The weaknesses of the Kuyperian model and the way in which it has been distorted in the South African setting lead us to ask about the possible corrective influence of the Barthian point of view. Although, as we have pointed out, Barthian theology was a late starter in Afrikaner Reformed thinking, it is making an impact. During the late 1960s and in the 1970s the church was referred to as an "alternative community" or an "alternative society," and in the open letter of 1982 addressed to the Dutch Reformed Church and drawn up by theologians of Dutch Reformed origin the Barthian influence is clearly seen.[13] In this letter the prophetic witness of the church *as* church is emphasized with reference to the following concrete issues: the alienating effect of apartheid upon the peoples of South Africa, the prohibition of mixed marriages, the system of racial classification, Group Areas, the forced removals of people, and so forth. Further, the church is also called God's "experimental garden." Through the life of the church God wishes to show what he intends for the whole of society as far as unity, mutual love, peace, a charitable spirit, and justice are concerned.

Finally, during the early 1980s, a further dimension of Karl Barth's thought on the relationship between church and society was gradually brought into the ongoing debate: that is, the idea that the church must side with the weak and the poor while it strives for social justice. It would be wrong, however, to assume that this idea was introduced into Afrikaner Reformed circles by the writings of Barth.[14] Few within these circles really paid attention to this aspect of Barth's thinking. Liberation theology introduced the concept of God's solidarity, and therefore the church's solidarity, with the poor and the oppressed. Only after the introduction of this idea, with the sharp controversy that it caused in theological circles, was it "discovered" that Barth had voiced this opinion many years before the advent of liberation theology.[15] For quite a few Afrikaner Reformed theologians this "discovery" came as a welcome support in their uphill struggle. For that matter, Kuyper himself could have been a prime witness in this regard, taking into consideration his very genuine social awareness.[16]

Despite these welcome corrections from a Barthian perspective, the obvious weaknesses in this model laid it open to attacks from different quarters, the most important criticism being against the assumption that society can and will imitate what happens inside the church and that the church can influence society accordingly. The power and influence of the church in this direction is hopelessly overestimated, the more so because the members of the church participate in the political and societal struggle *anonymously*.

That the Word of God should be preached in all concreteness does not imply that the individual believer is relieved of his or her duty to apply the Word to his own particular situation or to make his or her own political decisions, whether as ruler or subject. This is something the church cannot do for the individual. Thus, strengthened by the ministry of the Word on Sunday, the Christian should strive to be the salt of the earth on Monday, politically, socially, and economically. For that matter, the individual Christian may even organize a political party. The voice of the political party, however, can never substitute for the prophetic voice of the church. We should bear in mind that the difficulties experienced in the field of practical politics more often than not force Christians and so-called Christian political parties to compromise while applying the "art of the possible." The Word of God, however, can never be compromised and it is the responsibility of the church to proclaim the Word without compromise through prophetic ministry. To reiterate, as with any prophecy, an uncompromising word cannot be abstract. A prophetic voice that is not concrete is no prophetic voice at all. This much at least of Karl Barth's message has come to be accepted within influential South African theological circles as a genuine Reformed concept.

Of course no one denies the hermeneutical problem inherent in such a concept of the prophetic task of the church vis-à-vis the state. The more concrete the prophecy, the greater the danger that the specific situation and political considerations play an overriding role in the interpretation of Scripture. But the fact that this danger exists does not relieve the church of its duty.

The one danger the church should avoid, however, is to prescribe a certain political, social, or economic system. Such favoritism has nothing to do with a prophetic ministry. The church has to proclaim the prophetic Word of God, which contains in the first instance the message of God's acts of salvation through Jesus Christ. Although it is clear from the Bible that this salvation carries implications for every sphere of life, and although the Bible itself relates its message to specific and concrete situations, it never does so in the sense of prescribing a political or social program.

This unwillingness of the Bible to prescribe specific programs and systems on the one hand, and its critical attitude with regard to the structures of society on the other hand, correspond to the "not yet" and the "already" of the kingdom of God. The "not yet" carries within itself an eschatological reserve. It makes it clear that the kingdom is still to come and that it is presumptuous of the church to believe that it can bring about the kingdom by deducing principles from Scripture

135

and prescribing to the community a complete social and political program. The church is the bridgehead of the kingdom and the citizens of that kingdom constitute the church, but the church is not identical with the kingdom.

The "already" of the kingdom and the acknowledgment of the Lordship of Jesus Christ by the citizens of the kingdom, however, demands complete and uncompromising obedience to him. Therefore the church cannot rest content with the structures of this world. Its attitude remains basically critical.

In the practical arena of state and politics, what has been said means *inter alia* that Christians must strive to be uncompromisingly obedient to the Lord, knowing that they will be forced to compromise because the kingdom has not yet come. They may be able to erect signs of the coming kingdom, to push constantly at the edges of the possible, but they will not be able to do more than that. This fact, however, does not imply the church's capitulation to the inevitable. As we have said before, the prophetic message of the church is a constant reminder to all people that *it* cannot come to rest in the structures of this world.

The upshot is that the relation of the church to the state will of necessity be more critical than prescriptive. This may sound negative, but it is the only way in which the church can remain true to itself while refusing to compromise its own message. For the church to prescribe practical politics in the sense of supplying political alternatives is the surest way for it either to become irrelevant or to compromise its message. However, this critical stance should not prevent the church from praising and participating in actions where it sees signs of the kingdom being erected in ways consonant with the gospel. Furthermore, we should realize that this apparently negative function of the church is the direct outcome of the most positive of all messages: the proclamation that Christ is Lord of all life.

Taking a critical position does not, of course, mean that the church will erect foolproof safeguards against transgressing the necessary boundaries between church and state. The church has to ask itself continuously what God expects of it in a given situation. In extreme circumstances it might even be necessary for the church to exceed its normal limits for the sake of the kingdom. For instance, within the black communities of South Africa, the churches are sometimes the only public and therefore political mouthpieces for the people in their misery. If they are silent, only the stones can still cry out. Karl Barth would have recognized this need for the church occasionally to overstep its normal limits, because for him the church-state relationship was never static, but a dynamic process in which the church can never abdicate from its role as prophet or shrug off its responsibility to intercede for the poor and the voiceless who are in need.

Racism, Reconciliation, and Resistance

John W. de Gruchy

By way of introduction allow me the liberty of sharing two memories. The first is the memory of an editorial in a South African denominational magazine, *The Congregationalist,* written in the early 1950s. The editor was bemoaning the fact that so many Dutch Reformed ministers in South Africa supported apartheid. No wonder, he argued, because if you visited their studies you would see that their bookshelves are lined with Calvinist volumes, including many by Karl Barth! The second is the memory of hearing Professor B. B. Keet deliver a lecture on the occasion of the centenary of the Dutch Reformed theological seminary at Stellenbosch in 1959. He chose as his theme the development of Dutch Reformed theology during the past hundred years.[1] In the course of the lecture he dealt extensively with the influence of Karl Barth, expressing the hope that in spite of some points of relatively minor disagreement, the Dutch Reformed church would respond positively to Barth's challenge.

It is worth pondering upon these two reactions to Karl Barth. The first was by an English-speaking minister in the liberal tradition who failed to distinguish Barth either from Calvinist theologians of the past or, more seriously, from those neo-Calvinist theologians who provided theological legitimation for apartheid. The second, by a distinguished Dutch Reformed theologian by then already well known for his strong critique of apartheid, demonstrated an awareness of Barth's significance for the revitalizing of Reformed theology and the witness of the church against racism in South Africa.[2] The church struggle in South Africa has since shown that, of the two, Keet's perception was correct.

Barth's theology, however, cannot be regurgitated in our context as though it provides us with a ready-made theology that simply needs to be repeated. Such Barthianism is unhelpful and contradicts Barth's own understanding of theology as a task that has to be undertaken afresh in every new situation. Indeed, the very nature of Barth's theology—its polemical beginnings and its development in fresh directions over a long period of time—should make us wary of regurgitation. We need, rather, to keep firmly in mind Eberhard Jungel's dictum that "theology can only honour Karl Barth by steadfastly 'doing its thing.'"[3] Our task is to listen carefully to the Word of God as this Word speaks to us today, and insofar as Barth's theology enables us to do this better, we need to integrate his insights into what we have to do.

My own conviction is that Barth must be appropriated in South Africa in two ways. First, we must take seriously the radicality of his Christology, demonstrated, for example, in his unequivocal rejection of Nazism at Barmen. Second, we must be in discussion with the way in which that Christology is developed, especially in the doctrine of reconciliation in his *Church Dogmatics*. On the one hand, Barth provides us with resources for radically challenging those theologies that legitimate injustice and oppression; on the other hand, he provides us with an alternative theology for the church and its public responsibility. With this in mind, I have chosen to explore three themes: racism and the confession of Jesus Christ; reconciliation and the liberation of the oppressed; and resistance and the prayer of the church.

Racism and the Confession of Jesus Christ

In 1925 Barth addressed the World Alliance of Reformed Churches meeting in Cardiff on "The Desirability and Possibility of a Universal Reformed Creed." In general, Barth was skeptical because he felt that the Reformed churches were neither theologically nor contextually in a position where they could confess their faith anew, and, moreover, he believed they were unwilling do so concretely and relevantly. Nevertheless, Barth counseled:

> A church which today desired to confess its faith must have the courage to express the insight currently won from Scripture on the problems of life which *today* beset its members. It cannot wait until its statement comes thirty years too late, like the Social Manifesto of the Bielefeld Church Assembly. It must act while the problem is still "hot," while the Church can speak its word upon it where the word of the Church belongs, at the outset of the problem. The Church must have the courage to speak today upon the fascist, racialist *nationalism*

which since the war is appearing in similar forms in all countries. Does the Church say yes or no to this nationalism?[4]

By the early 1930s, however, Barth, along with Dietrich Bonhoeffer, recognized that the time had definitely come when the church could no longer remain silent on the matter, especially in Germany. A *status confessionis* had arrived, requiring the church to declare anew and unequivocally in the most concrete possible way that Jesus Christ is Lord. For Barth as for Bonhoeffer, this meant the rejection of National Socialism and its Aryan program as anti-Christian.

There can be no doubt that the Barmen Declaration and the story of the Confessing Church struggle in Germany, especially the witness of Barth and Bonhoeffer, have decisively influenced the church struggle in South Africa during the past twenty-five years.[5] It is doubtful whether we in South Africa would ever have come to the realization that a *status confessionis* does exist in our situation, and that apartheid must be rejected as a heresy, unless we had had before us their testimony and were able to learn from their theological insight. Of course, this has not meant that we simply have had the task of reaffirming the Barmen Declaration. Rather, as Barth himself taught, we have had the task of confessing Jesus Christ concretely in terms that relate directly to our situation. This is the significance of *The Message to the People of South Africa* (1968); the Belhar Confession of Faith (1982) of the Dutch Reformed Mission Church; as well as the latest and most radical of all theological attacks upon apartheid, the Kairos Document (1985).

Barth makes only one reference to South Africa in his writings, namely, in *Church Dogmatics* (IV/1, 703). By the time South Africa had become a subject of widespread debate after Sharpeville, Barth was already on the brink of retirement. However, he was certainly aware of the problem of apartheid and was undoubtedly concerned about the role of the church in relation to it. He expressed his concern sharply and with characteristic terseness in the Annexure to Ben Marais's book *Colour: the Unsolved Problem of the West*, published in 1952.[6] Marais had written to several well-known international theologians asking for their response to a number of questions bearing on race relations. Barth was one who responded. The questions, and Barth's answers (which were the shortest of all by far), read as follows:

(1)

Do you believe that the Old Testament record of the relationship between Israel and the heathens can in any sense serve as a directive for: (a) The mutual relationship between different nations today? (b) The relationship between church and nation?

(a) No!

(b) Yes!

(2)

Does the Bible, according to your view, prescribe, permit, or prohibit a "volkskerk" (in the sense of an ethnical church)?

Prohibit!

(3)

Does the Bible leave scope for a separate church organization for different national, racial, cultural and social groups who inhabit the same territory or residential area?

No!

(4)

If you answer 3 in the affirmative, do you also believe that the Bible gives justification or leaves scope for a policy of *enforced* racial segregation within the Christian church?

No!

(5)

(a) If according to your view the Bible gives such justification, do you believe that it can be stretched to the point where for instance a non-white believer is debarred, on grounds of race or colour, from joining a white church or white congregation? (b) Name the Scriptural ground or grounds, if any, on which you believe such a policy can be based.

No!

(6)

"A policy of enforced racial segregation within the Christian church can be justified on the ground that God will separate races and nations, each with a different language, culture, etc., and therefore racial segregation (even within the Christian church) so as to keep races intact, is not only permissible, but a Christian duty." Do you agree with this statement? Briefly comment, please.

No! Nazi-Theology!

(8)

"All racial mixture is against the will and ordinances of God." Do you subscribe to this view? Briefly comment, please.

No! Nazi-Theology!

Barth's responses to these questions leave one in no doubt that he categorically rejected any attempt to divide the church along racial or nationalist lines. Indeed, for Barth, the "earthly historical form" of the church, its *Gestalt,* was, as the third thesis of the Barmen Declaration indicated, part of its confession of Jesus Christ. Thus, in his discussion in *Church Dogmatics* on the catholicity of the church, which contains his only reference to South Africa, Barth writes:

> How much longer will it be possible in the United States and South Africa to ratify the social distinctions between whites and blacks by a corresponding division in the Church, instead of calling it in question in the social sphere by the contrary practice of the church?[7]

Barth's response to the questions Marais posed also shows that he would have had no sympathy for the claim made by any nation, other than Israel, to have a favored place or role in the economy of God. The idea of a "manifest destiny" or of a special covenant made between a nation and God outside of the covenant made in Christ, such as between the Afrikaner nation and God at Blood River, would be totally unacceptable. Thus Barth was highly critical of British and German imperialism and, during the Third Reich, of National Socialism. What concerned him in particular was the messianic pretensions of such movements, their religious character and legitimation, and their pride in attempting to play God.

It was, of course, Barth's experience in the Third Reich that provided the background to his response to the questions raised by Ben Marais. Barth probably saw little difference between white racism and Nazi anti-Semitism; certainly both were to be condemned as anti-Christian. He therefore also attacked any attempt to provide a theological justification for them, whether it was to be found in the natural theology of liberal Protestantism or in the theologies of creation, orders, or spheres, which Lutherans and Calvinists used for this purpose. Hence Barth's critique of the neo-Calvinism of Abraham Kuyper, and, implicitly, of the way in which this has influenced the ideology of apartheid in South Africa. The first thesis of the Barmen Declaration is a clear rejection of both a liberal theology that allows itself to become the captive of bourgeois culture, and a confessional theology of creation that gives culture, nation, or race an ontological status.

Undergirding Barth's critique of these distortions of Christian faith and the misuse of God to legitimate racism or capitalism is his Christology. For Barth, the "God of the Bible" is not the "Almighty" to which Hitler and many other tyrants have paid lip-service, nor is this God the "tedious magnitude known as transcendence" that is "an illusory reflection of human freedom" projected "into the vacuum of utter abstraction."[8] The "God of the Bible" is the "Word made flesh" in Jesus Christ, and confession of this One Word (Barmen) must result in the rejection of every attempt to co-opt the name of God for the legitimation of ends contrary to the gospel. Such a confession does not simply imply the repeating of the name of Jesus Christ "as though it were a mantra," or of defending the Chalcedonian formula in some kind of ahistorical way.[9] Rather, it means confessing Jesus Christ as God's definitive Word on the concrete issues facing the church today.

While there are surprisingly few references in Barth's *Church Dogmatics* to the phenomenon and problem of racism as such, from beginning to end his theology stands in contradiction to it. Indeed, whether we consider his understanding of the covenant or the creation, his Christology, anthropology, or his ecclesiology, we soon discover that they all bear witness to God's reconciliation of all men and women and of their responsibility for each other. Human beings, according to Barth, are only human in this relationship to each other under God.[10]

In 1928, five years before he began to challenge the anti-Semitic racism of National Socialism, and long before Europeans in general in post–Second World War Europe even became aware of their relationship to colonial racism, Barth showed an existential awareness of the problem in his lectures on ethics. In examining the issues involved in the human need to appropriate things for the sake of "the will to live," he wrote:

> When members of the white race all enjoy every possible intellectual and material advantage on the basis of the superiority of one race and the subjection of many other races, and of the use that for centuries our race has made of both, I myself may not have harmed a single hair on the heads of Africans or Indians. I may be friendly toward them. I may be a supporter of missions. Yet I am still a member of the white race which, as a whole, has obviously used very radically the possibility of appropriation in relation to them. My share in the sin against Africa or Asia for the last hundred or fifty years may be very remote or indirect,

but would Europe be what it is, and would I be what I am, if that expansion had never happened?[11]

This very revealing comment shows Barth's awareness that racism is far more than simply a matter of bad education and social-psychology; it is inseparable from human greed, not only at the micro-economic level of a particular country but also at the macro-level of international trade. Barth's long-standing commitment to democratic socialism confirms that for him the problems of racism and economic injustice or poverty cannot be separated.

Reconciliation and the Liberation of the Oppressed

Already in 1969 the problem of the relationship between reconciliation and political liberation was raised by James Cone in his first study on black theology, *Black Theology and Black Power*.[12] In South Africa the debate continued for some time but has now heated up considerably with the Kairos Document's rejection of the way in which reconciliation is misused in what it calls "Church Theology."

> In our situation in South Africa today it would be totally unChristian to plead for reconciliation and peace before the present injustices have been removed. Any such plea plays into the hands of the oppressor by trying to persuade those of us who are oppressed to accept our oppression and to become reconciled to the intolerable crimes that are committed against us. That is not Christian reconciliation, it is sin. It is asking us to become accomplices in our own oppression, to become servants of the devil. No reconciliation is possible in South Africa *without justice*. What this means in practice is that no reconciliation, no forgiveness and no negotiations are possible *without repentance*. The Biblical teaching on reconciliation and forgiveness makes it quite clear that nobody can be forgiven and reconciled with God unless he or she repents of their sins. Nor are *we* expected to forgive the unrepentant sinner. When he or she repents we must be willing to forgive seventy times seven times, but before that, we are expected to preach repentance to those who sin against us or against anyone. Reconciliation, forgiveness and negotiations will become our Christian duty in South Africa only when the apartheid regime shows genuine repentance.[13]

There can be no question that at one level this understanding of reconciliation is biblical. The Bible does not teach, as Bonhoeffer would say, "cheap reconciliation," reconciliation without repentance. Moreover, the Bible does not separate reconciliation to God from reconciliation with "our brother" (Matt. 5:23-24). The question is, What is the relationship between this message of reconciliation to God and "our brother," and sociopolitical reconciliation and liberation? Are they to be equated, and, if not, how are they to be related or distinguished?

Barth's doctrine of reconciliation was firmly grounded in his Christology, and it is precisely his Christology that enables him to distinguish and yet affirm an intrinsic relationship between reconciliation with God and sociopolitical liberation. Just as for Barth there is a very close connection between reconciliation and justification, and between justification and social justice, so he dialectically related the gospel of God's reconciliation to the establishment of a just peace in the world.

While ultimately, or eschatologically, reconciliation and a just social peace are the same, penultimately—that is, "in between the times"—they cannot be equated. Hence Barth's eschatological reservation that prevents him, and rightly so, from equating sociopolitical solutions with the coming kingdom of God. At best such solutions can only partially point to what is yet to come. Nevertheless, the fact that they can do this is of fundamental importance, because what is at stake here is the provisional approximation to the coming kingdom, the present though incomplete realization of God's reconciliation in Christ in the midst of the world. As Jürgen Moltmann correctly interprets Barth,

> The Christian community wants the state to point toward the kingdom of God, not away from it. It wants God's grace also to be reflected in the external, temporary dealings of the political community.[14]

For Barth, God's reconciliation of the world to himself has taken place in and through the incarnation, death, and resurrection of Jesus Christ. This is an objective "given." This act of reconciliation, in a profound sense, precedes rather than follows the creation and fall of humanity, as more traditional theologians teach. For Barth, the Christian community or church is the "provisional representation" of the sanctification of all humanity, and therefore of God's reconciliation of the world to himself.

> The goal in the direction of which the true Church proceeds and moves is the revelation of the sanctification of all humanity and human life as it has already taken place *de jure* in Jesus Christ. In the exaltation of the one Jesus, who as the Son of God became a servant in order as such to become the Lord of all men, there has been accomplished already in powerful archetype, not only the cancellation of the sins and there-

fore the justification, but also the elevation and establishment of all humanity and human life and therefore its sanctification. That this is the case is the theme and content of the witness with which his community is charged. It comes from the first revelation (in the resurrection of Jesus Christ) of the reconciliation of the world with God as it has taken place in this sense too.[15]

The fundamental difference between the church and the world is that the former recognizes, acknowledges, confesses, and seeks to express God's reconciliation in Jesus Christ in its life, whereas the world fails to recognize and acknowledge what God has in fact done. The church's task is therefore to enable the world to discover the reality of God's reconciliation in Christ, and to express it, however inadequately, here and now in society.[16] The church is thus a sign of the new humanity that God is creating in Christ, having broken down the walls that divide the human race into warring factions.

The Kairos Document is surely right in maintaining that there is an integral relationship between God's gift of reconciliation in Christ and sociopolitical liberation, and that therefore a politics of repentance and forgiveness is essential if human society is to be transformed. It may, of course, be debated as to whether forgiveness comes before or after repentance, whether it is a means to repentance or its consequence, or better, whether the two are related in a far less causal manner. But the Kairos Document is correct in requiring that those who have perpetrated the injustices and suffering of apartheid should acknowledge their guilt if there is to be genuine reconciliation and peace in South Africa. Dietrich Bonhoeffer saw this so clearly in Germany, and, in fact, required the church to become the vicarious representative of the nation in this regard. That is why the call by some Dutch Reformed Church theologians in South Africa for a confession of guilt is so significant.

A possible danger of the Kairos Document is that it does not make the distinction between the church and the world clear enough, and therefore fails to distinguish adequately between God's gift of reconciliation that we can already celebrate and express, and the attempt to work out political solutions and structures in a very fallen world. Christians are reconciled to God and one another by virtue of the death and resurrection of Jesus Christ. The problem to which the Kairos Document bears witness is that many Christians in South Africa refuse to express this gift of reconciliation in practice precisely because of the costly change it requires. Nevertheless for Barth, it is not repentance that makes reconciliation possible but God's reconciling work in Christ that makes repentance and therefore liberation possible. The situation is analogous to the unity God has given in Christ to the church, a gift that can be denied and squandered rather than demonstrated. The task of the church is to bear witness to that reconciliation in such a way that it becomes a transforming message in society and not a cop-out.

How, then, is the church to proclaim the gospel of reconciliation so that it enables rather than hinders the process of just social transformation and liberation? Barth would undoubtedly respond that the task of the church in this regard is simply to be the church, that is, to demonstrate in the world the power of the gospel.[17] But Barth did not understand this as the church being neutral in the political struggle for justice and liberation. He makes it very clear time and again that the church has to take sides, another affinity he shares with the Kairos Document. Consider, for example, this passage from the *Church Dogmatics* (II/1), where Barth is discussing the mercy and righteousness of God:

> God always takes his stand unconditionally and passionately on this side and on this side alone: against the lofty and on behalf of the lowly; against those who already enjoy right and privilege and on behalf of those who are denied it and deprived of it. What does all this mean? It is not really to be explained by talking *in abstracto* of the political tendency and especially the forensic character of the Old Testament and the biblical message generally. It does in fact have this character and we cannot hear it and believe it without feeling a sense of responsibility in the direction indicated. As a matter of fact, from the belief in God's righteousness there follows logically a very definite political problem and task. . . .[18]

Or, as Barth wrote in his letter to the French Protestants in December 1939:

> Precisely because the Church knows about justification which we men cannot attain by any means for ourselves, she cannot remain indifferent. She cannot remain "neutral" in things great and small where justice is at stake, where the attempt is being made to establish a poor feeble human justice over against overwhelming, flagrant injustice.[19]

The righteousness and mercy of God, which is the basis of our reconciliation, thus lead us to take a stand on behalf of the poor and oppressed, and in solidarity with them, to struggle for justice and liberation.

Resistance and the Prayer of the Church

The relationship between the state and those churches in South Africa that have opposed apartheid since 1948 has become increasingly strained and problematic over the years. The almost built-in tension between so-called English-speaking churches and an Afrikaner Nationalist government, derived from a long history of cultural and political conflict between the Afrikaner and the English in South Africa, has been exacerbated by, *inter alia,* the WCC Programme to Combat Racism, the "radicalization" of the SACC and its member churches, support for those engaged in certain forms of civil disobedience and for the day of prayer to end unjust rule, and most recently by the Harare Declaration of the South African member churches of the WCC.

The so-called English-speaking churches are, of course, politically divided and polarized within themselves, so their stand against apartheid is often ambiguous and reluctant, and their theology, as the Kairos Document maintains, may even serve the interests of the *status quo.* At the same time, since the majority of their members are black, these churches are supportive (at least officially as institutions) of those who are struggling to bring about just social transformation. Inevitably this stance on the side of those struggling for liberation, and sometimes direct involvement in the struggle, mean confrontation and often stormy conflict between church and state, even though it may be interspersed by lulls and attempts to relate more positively. Clearly the state security apparatus regards such churches as a threat to the security of the state, and much is done to discredit their work and ministry.

In such a situation it becomes crucial that the church continually assess its role in society and, more specifically, its responsibility toward the state. Barth's understanding of the relationship between church and state, especially as stated in his essays "Gospel and Law" (1935), "Church and State" or (better) "Rechtfertigung und Recht" (1938), and "Christian Community and Civil Community" (1946), helps considerably in clarifying the issues.

In "Rechtfertigung und Recht," written against the background of Nazi Germany, Barth's major concern is to show the relationship between the Reformation teaching on justification by faith and the political responsibility of the church in the struggle for justice. For Barth, the Reformers implied a connection and demonstrated that the two are not in conflict with each other. However, they failed to make the connection clearly and draw out its practical implications. Indeed, when they began to talk about the political responsibility and task of the church they appealed more to the law than to the gospel. A serious consequence of this separation of law and gospel, and the development of political ethics on the basis of law rather than gospel, has been the pietistic withdrawal of vast sections of the church from any political responsibility or involvement in the struggle for justice. This has been particularly true in South Africa, especially among white Christians. Justification before God has been separated from the pursuit of God's justice in the world. Thus, Barth asks, "is there an actual, and therefore inward and vital, connection between the two realms?"[20] In a situation where psuedo-piety within both the church and the state has kept these two realms strictly apart, this question is of fundamental importance.

Barth approaches the problem, as usual, from a christological perspective. He reflects, first of all, on the encounter between Jesus and Pilate, which, he maintains, not only teaches the separation of church and state but also confirms the power of the state as something given by God, a power that "even in this 'demonic' form" can render service. While Pilate's handing of Jesus over to death is a failure by the state to execute justice, in a more profound sense it is fulfilling God's purposes of justification. Hence the need to give the state the honor that is due to it not only by virtue of its God-given authority but also by virtue of the fact that at this critical moment in the drama of redemption, in God's justification of the sinner, the state fulfills a fundamental role. "Pontius Pilate now belongs not only to the Creed but to its second article in particular!"[21] In other words, we must approach the problem of church and state christologically rather than on the basis of a theology of creation as in the German Lutheranism of Barth's day or the neo-Calvinism that has so deeply influenced Afrikaner Nationalism.

Barth approaches the problem in another way by examining Romans 13:1-7, which, as the Kairos Document points out, has been so misused in South Africa in support of the *status quo* and against those churches and Christians who are critical of the state. Contrary to such abuse, Barth maintains that "the last thing this instruction implies is that the Christian community and the Christian should offer the blindest possible obedience to the civil community and its officials." He continues:

> What is meant is (Rom. 13.6f.) that Christians should carry out what is required of them for the establishment, preservation and maintenance of the civil community and for the execution of its task, be-

cause, although they are Christians and, as such, have their home elsewhere, they also live in this outer circle. Jesus Christ is still its centre:
they too are responsible for its stability.[22]

It is important to note Barth's final comment that Christians are responsible for the stability of society and that this is said within the
context of refusing to give to civil authority any blind unqualified allegiance.

Barth's exegesis and discussion of Romans 13:1-7 in "Rechfer-
tigung und Recht," though not beyond criticism,[23] shows, further, that
we must understand the passage in relation to the fact that the state can
and often does change character.

> Thus there is clearly no cause for the Church to act as though it lived,
> in relation to the State, in a night in which all cats are grey. It is much
> more a question of continual decisions, and therefore of distinctions
> between one State and another, between the State of yesterday and the
> State of today.[24]

It is therefore quite crucial for the church, in relating to the state, to be
able to discern the state's character at any given time. Is it exercising
its God-given responsibility for good or for evil, that is, in ways consonant with or contrary to the Lordship of Jesus Christ? Although the
church will always relate to the state in such a way as upholds the
God-given authority of the state, the precise manner in which this is
done will depend upon the answer to this question and not on the basis
of some ontological status given to the state in creation.

In submitting to the authority of the state, then, the church is dealing indirectly with the authority of Jesus Christ the Redeemer; it is, in
other words, a response that is related to justification before God. It is
Jesus Christ the Lord and King who, after all, gives the state its
authority. Thus, Barth writes:

> In the decisions of the State the Church will always support the side
> which clarifies rather than obscures the Lordship of Jesus Christ over
> the whole, which includes this political sphere outside the Church.
> The Church desires that the shape and reality of the State in this fleet-
> ing world should point towards the Kingdom of God, not away from
> it. Its desire is not that human politics should cross the politics of God,
> but that they should proceed, however distantly, on parallel lines.[25]

While Barth did not believe that social democracy could ever be
equated with the coming kingdom of God, he did believe that it was
more in line with the kingdom than were other forms of government.

Barth is quite clear that there should be no confusion between the role of the church and that of the state, and that neither should try to usurp the role of the other. He is equally clear that the church cannot expect the state to bring in the kingdom of God and establish a utopia. But this does not mean that the church has no responsibility in directing and enabling the state toward the coming of God's kingdom. On the contrary. The Christian lives in anticipation of the coming kingdom of God, that is, a new political order. All political structures, therefore, including the state itself, are transient and not final. "It is the hope of the new age, which is dawning in power, that separates the Church from the State, that is, from the States of this age and this world."[26] Thus, as Barth states many times, the greatest service the church can render the state is for it to be the church.[27]

The church is always a stranger on earth because it is anticipating that which is to come. In proclaiming the kingdom of God, God's righteousness and justification, the church is not claiming to be the new order, nor is it denying the right of the state to exist and exercise its authority; rather, the church is proclaiming its hope, witnessing to the transient character of the present order, expressing its qualified and critical rather than unconditional obedience to the state. Therefore, the more the state claims to be absolute the more the church is in conflict with it. The church cannot claim to be the state, but neither can the state claim to be the church and in the name of God legitimate its policies.

Barth accepts the need, then, for the Christian to pay taxes as he also accepts the need for the Christian to participate in the military and defend the state when it is unjustly threatened. But he categorically rejects any right the state may claim to demand of its citizens and therefore of the church a particular *Weltanschauung,* imposed from without (i.e., by the state).

> When the State begins to claim "love," it is in the process of becoming a Church, the Church of a false God, and thus an unjust State. The just State requires, not love, but a simple, resolute, and responsible attitude on the part of its citizens.[28]

It is noteworthy, especially in relation to the End Conscription debate in South Africa today, that in his 1928 lectures on ethics Barth could say:

> Ethically, the most dangerous form of participation in war is not, then, that of service in the infantry, the artillery, or even the poison-gas corps, but undoubtedly that of the chaplains' service, because this is the place where it is so uncannily easy to betray the cause of ethics

publicly and to promote that evil ideology instead of ethical reflection.[29]

Indeed, the church has to oppose any attempt by the state to try to play the role of the church. It is against such a claim that the Kairos Document has been so outspoken and critical. "State Theology," the document claims, misuses "theological concepts and biblical texts for its own political purposes." One example of this is "the use of the idea of 'Law and Order' to determine and control what the people may be permitted to regard as just and unjust" (Introduction to Chapter 2). The church surrenders its responsibility when it allows the state to become the arbiter of what is right and just. For when the state determines what is "just or unjust" it also takes to itself the power to determine the nature of "Law and Order." What the state calls "Law and Order" may well be, from the perspective of the gospel, unjust disorder that the church must oppose on the grounds of what it perceives to be God's justice. Precisely because the church is concerned about stability and genuine law and order within society, it must refuse to abnegate its responsibility to discern what is just and unjust in the light of the gospel. Law and order is always contingent upon justice. Thus when the church confronts the state it must be because the state is failing to exercise justice and therefore maintain law and order. Barth sums this up by saying:

> The Church always stands for the constitutional State, for the maximum validity and application of that twofold rule (no exemption from and full protection by the law), and therefore it will always be against any degeneration of the constitutional State into tyranny or anarchy. The Church will never be found on the side of anarchy or tyranny. In its politics it will always be urging the civil community to treat this fundamental purpose of its existence with the utmost seriousness: the limiting and preserving of man by the quest for and the establishment of law.[30]

It is within this context alone that we can understand Barth's insistence upon the service of the church toward the state as resistance and prayer, and to see that these two are not poles apart but belong together. As Barth put it in the final fragment of his *Church Dogmatics*, in the church's struggle for human righteousness it has to "revolt against disorder."[31]

Barth regards intercession for the state as the primary task of the church in relation to the state. This means praying for the welfare of those in authority, that they will be enabled to exercise their authority justly. But it also is a reminder that their authority is derived from God and not themselves. Prayer for the state is a reminder of the limits to its authority. This task of intercession becomes more urgent and necessary the more the state becomes unjust, opposes the preaching of God's righteousness and justification, and thereby destroys and annuls itself.[32] Indeed, the church's opposition to an unjust state is not an action against the state, it is service rendered on behalf of the state.

> Christians would be neglecting the distinctive service which they can and must render to the State, were they to adopt an attitude of unquestioning assent to the will and action of the State which is directly or indirectly aimed at the suppression of the freedom of the Word of God. For the possibility of intercession for the State stands or falls within the freedom of God's Word. Christians would, in point of fact, become enemies of any State if, when the State threatens their freedom, they did *not* resist, or if they concealed their resistance—although this resistance would be very calm and dignified. . . . If the State has perverted its God-given authority, it cannot be honoured better than by this *criticism* which is due to it in all circumstances.[33]

In this way the church's witness preserves the state; "it defends the state against the state," even though political control of the state may change. It is precisely in this sense that we must understand the call by the SACC in 1985 to pray for a change of government in South Africa.[34] Such prayer is on behalf of the state, not against it, because it is prayer that God's kingdom will "come on earth as in heaven." And, as Barth wrote to the French Protestants in 1940, such *"prayer* will not lead us away from political thought and action of a modest but definite kind, but will rather lead us directly into purposeful conflict."[35]

While intercession is at the heart of this service, it cannot be separated from action.

> Can we ask God for something which we are not at the same moment determined and prepared to bring about, so far as it lies within the bounds of our possibility? Can we pray that the State shall preserve us, and that it may continue to do so as a just State, or that it will again become a just State, and not at the same time pledge ourselves personally, both in thought and action, in order that this may happen, without sharing the earnest desire of the Scottish Confession and saying, with it: *Vitae bonorum adesse, tyrranidem opprimere, ab infirmioribus vim improborum defender* ("to save the lives of the innocent, to repress tyranny, to defend the oppressed"), thus, without, in certain cases, like Zwingli, reckoning with the possibility of revolution, the possibility, according to his strong expression, that we may have to "overthrow with God" those rulers who do not follow the lines laid

down by Christ? Can we give the State that respect which is its due without making its business our own, with *all* the consequences that this implies?[36]

The church has, therefore, the awesome responsibility of discerning the character of the state and thereby determining what its response should be in each historical circumstance. The response always arises out of its witness to the gospel and therefore its calling to be the church, but what that prayer and action may be will depend upon the face that the state adopts. Christian perceptions of the state in South Africa vary a great deal depending on one's social location. For some the state is presently governed by a Christian government, for others it is a tyrannt (Kairos Document), and there are various positions in between. If, as many of us believe, apartheid and all that goes with it are essentially destructive of human life, and therefore a form of disorder not order, lawlessness not law, then it becomes the duty of the church to resist it and through prayer and action work toward the transformation of society along lines that lead toward the coming kingdom of God, even if that must always be beyond our human endeavors.

Notes

Notes to
Introduction: Reclaiming the Christian Heritage

1. J. de Gruchy and C. Villa-Vicencio, eds., *Apartheid is a Heresy* (Cape Town: David Philip; Grand Rapids: Eerdmans, 1981), 59-74.

2. See Appendix in ibid.

3. J. H. Cone, *My Soul Looks Back* (Maryknoll, N.Y.: Orbis Books, 1986), 60.

4. J. Habermas, *Knowledge and Human Interests* (Boston: Beacon Books, 1971).

5. J. Míguez-Bonino, *Toward a Christian Political Ethics* (Philadelphia: Fortress Press, 1983), 43.

6. Ibid., 43-44.

7. Both these documents are appended in C. Villa-Vicencio, *Between Christ and Caesar: Classical and Contemporary Texts* (Grand Rapids: Eerdmans; Cape Town: David Philip, 1986).

8. R. R. Reuther, "Augustine and Christian Political Theology," *Interpretation* 29 (1975): 252-65.

9. K. Barth, *The Knowledge of God and the Service of God* (London: Hodder & Stoughton, 1938); Barth, *Learning Jesus Christ Through the Heidelberg Catechism* (Grand Rapids: Eerdmans, 1984).

10. J. Dillenberger and C. Welch, *Protestant Christianity Interpreted Through Its Development* (New York: Charles Scribner's Sons, 1954), 89.

11. J. W. Beardslee, ed., *Reformed Dogmatics* (Grand Rapids: Baker, 1977), 4-10.

12. Dillenberger and Welch, "Protestant Christianity," 97.

13. J. W. de Gruchy, *The Church Struggle in South Africa* (Grand Rapids: Eerdmans; Cape Town: David Philip, 1979).

14. C. Villa-Vicencio and J. W. de Gruchy, eds., *Resistance and Hope: South African Essays in Honor of Beyers Naudé* (Cape Town: David Philip; Grand Rapids: Eerdmans, 1985), 39-51.

15. A. Kuyper, *Lectures on Calvinism* (Grand Rapids: Eerdmans, 1970), 90-99.

16. Durand, in Villa-Vicencio and de Gruchy, eds., *Resistance and Hope,*

40. See also Durand's essay in this volume, "Church and State in South Africa: Karl Barth vs. Abraham Kuyper."

17. B. Moore, ed., *Essays in Black Theology* (Atlanta: John Knox Press, 1973).

18. See the discussion in J. W. de Gruchy, "The Revitalization of Calvinism in South Africa: Some Reflections on Christian Belief, Theology, and Social Transformation," *The Journal of Religious Ethics* 14 (Spring 1986).

19. José Míguez-Bonino, "Historical Praxis and Christian Identity," in *Frontiers of Theology in Latin America,* ed. Rosino Gibellini (Maryknoll, N.Y.: Orbis Books, 1979), 263-72. This matter is further discussed in my essay, "Karl Barth's Revolution of God: Quietism or Anarchy?" included in this volume.

20. John Deschner, "Karl Barth as Political Activist," *Union Seminary Quarterly Review* 28 (Fall 1972): 55.

21. This incident is told by Edward Huenemann. The graduate student referred to is Frederick Herzog, presently a professor at Duke University.

22. See B. B. Keet in *Christian Principles in a Multi-Racial South Africa: A Report of the DRC Conference of Church Leaders,* Pretoria, 1953, 176-77. See also his *Suid Afrika Waarheen?* (Stellenbosch, 1956), 85.

23. B. B. Keet, "Honderd Jaar in Voelvlug," *Nederduitse Gereformeerde Teologies Tydskrif* 1 (1959): 5-13.

24. B. B. Keet, "The Bell Has Already Tolled," in *Delayed Action* (Pretoria: NG Kerkboekhandel, 1961).

25. C. Villa-Vicencio, "Theology in the Service of the State: the Steyn and Eloff Commissions," in Villa-Vicencio and de Gruchy, eds., *Resistance and Hope,* 113.

26. See, for example, Neuhaus's discussion with Johan Heyns in R. J. Neuhaus, *Dispensations: The Future of South Africa as South Africans See It* (Grand Rapids: Eerdmans, 1986), 27.

27. G. Ebeling, *Word and Faith* (Philadelphia: Fortress Press, 1963), 358.

Notes to
Paradigms of Radical Grace

1. D. J. Smit, "In a Special Way the God of the Destitute, the Poor and the Wronged," in *A Moment of Truth: The Confession of the Dutch Reformed Mission Church,* ed. G. D. Cloete and D. J. Smit (Grand Rapids: Eerdmans, 1984), 53-65, 127-50.

2. J. B. Thompson, *Studies in the Theory of Ideology* (Cambridge: Polity Press, 1984).

3. M. L. Stackhouse, *Creeds, Societies, and Human Rights: A Study in Three Cultures* (Grand Rapids: Eerdmans, 1984).

4. See S. Maimela, "Denominationalism—An Embarrassment for the Church," in *Denominationalism: Its Sources and Implications,* ed. W. S. Vorster (Pretoria: UNISA, 1982), 1-11.

5. To mention only two: J. de Gruchy, *The Church Struggle in South Africa* (Grand Rapids: Eerdmans; Cape Town: David Philip, 1979); C. Villa-Vicencio

and J. de Gruchy, eds., *Resistance and Hope* (Grand Rapids: Eerdmans; Cape Town: David Philip, 1985).

6. Two interesting examples from other contexts are J. D. Bratt, *Dutch Calvinism in Modern America: A History of a Conservative Subculture* (Grand Rapids: Eerdmans, 1984), and R. A. Alves, *Protestantism and Repression: A Brazilian Case Study* (London: SCM, 1985).

7. J. Pelikan, *The Christian Tradition: Reformation of Church and Dogma*, vol. 4 (Chicago: University of Chicago Press, 1984), 127-82.

8. See the instructive comparison between different confessional views in O. Jager, "Is de Incarnatie méér dan een 'Noodmaatregel'?" in *Rondom het Woord*, vol. 10, no. 1 (1968): 71-102.

9. A. Dulles, *Models of the Church* (New York: Doubleday, 1978).

10. K. Barth, *The Christian Life: Lecture Fragments* (Grand Rapids: Eerdmans, 1981).

11. See, for example, B. Klappert's definitive study on Barth's Christology, *Die Auferweckung des Gekreuzigten*. T. A. Mofokeng, *The Crucified among the Crossbearers* (Kampen: Kok, 1983), has also focused on par. 64, in comparison with par. 59, analyzing the importance of Barth's Christology, especially the place of the "cross," to develop a Black Christology from the perspective of South African black people.

12. For this period in his life cf. the specific chapter in E. Busch, *Karl Barth: His Life from Letters and Autobiographical Texts* (Philadelphia: Fortress Press, 1976). Both lectures, "The Gift of Freedom" (21 Sept. 1953) and "The Humanity of God" (25 Sept. 1956), have been published in *The Humanity of God*, 2d ed. (London: Collins, 1971).

13. Durand uses this expression in the second edition of his *Die lewende God* (Pretoria: NG Kerkboekhandel, 1986), 109-10.

14. See Smit, "In a Special Way," 127-50, for a discussion of several of these traditions in the Bible.

15. G. C. Berkouwer, *The Triumph of Grace in the Theology of Karl Barth* (Grand Rapids: Eerdmans, 1956).

16. K. Barth, *Final Testimonies*, ed. E. Busch (Grand Rapids: Eerdmans, 1977), 29-30.

17. C. E. Braaten, *Principles of Lutheran Theology* (Philadelphia: Fortress Press, 1983), 75-78.

18. For two important studies on this crucial category of "freedom," see E. J. Beker, *Libertas. Een onderzoek naar de leer van de vrijheid bij Reinhold Niebuhr en bij Karl Barth* (Nijerk: G. F. Callenbach, 1958), and U. Hedinger, *Der Freiheitsbegriff in der Kirchlichen Dogmatik Karl Barths* (Zürich: Zwingli Verlag, 1962). Both of them pay attention to the implications for ethics as well.

19. Cf. W. Krötke, *Sünde und Nichtiges bei Karl Barth*, 2d ed. (Neukirchen-Vluyn: Neukirchener Verlag, 1983), esp. 104ff.

20. In the United States Reinhold Niebuhr, for example, called Barth "irrelevant to all Christians in the Western world who believe in accepting common and collective responsibilities without illusion and without despair" (*Christian Century*, vol. 77, no. 19 [1960]). The criticism in the Netherlands, from the side of the so-called neo-Calvinists, is well documented and analyzed in M. E. Brink-

man, *De theologie van Karl Barth: dynamiet of dynamo voor christelijk handelen* (Baarn: Ten Have, 1983). R. W. Lovin, *Christian Faith and Public Choices* (Philadelphia: Fortress Press, 1984), compares Barth, Brunner, and Bonhoeffer with a view to their relevance for making public choices.

21. W. Schlichting, *Biblische Denkform in der Dogmatik* (Zürich: Theologischer Verlag, 1971).

22. J. Gustafson, *Ethics from a Theocentric Perspective*, vol. 2: *Ethics and Theology* (Chicago: University of Chicago Press, 1984), 25-26.

23. R. E. Willis, *The Ethics of Karl Barth* (Leiden: E. J. Brill, 1971), 4.

24. C. C. West, "Karl Barth," in *A Dictionary of Christian Ethics,* ed. J. Macquarrie, 3d ed. (London: SCM, 1974), 27.

25. The concept of "analogy" is crucially important for Barth's thinking and his ethics. For a description of his change from dialectics to analogy, cf. E. Jüngel, "Von der Dialektik zur Analogie," in *Barth-Studien* (Gütersloh: Gerd Mohn, 1982), 127-79. For a well-known discussion of analogy in Barth's work, see H. G. Pöhlmann, *Analogia entis or Analogia fidei?* (Göttingen: Vandenhoeck & Ruprecht, 1965).

26. M. Honecker, "Karl Barth," in *Evangelisches Soziallexikon* (Stuttgart: Kreuz Verlag, 1980), 123-24.

27. G. W. Bromiley, *Introduction to the Theology of Karl Barth* (Grand Rapids: Eerdmans, 1979), 246.

28. For useful introductions to Reformed life and thought, see J. H. Leith, *Introduction to the Reformed Tradition,* 3d ed. (Atlanta: John Knox, 1981) and I. J. Hesselink, *On Being Reformed* (Ann Arbor: Servant Books, 1983).

Notes to
Karl Barth's Revolution of God

1. The above quotations are from the sections entitled "The Great Negative Possibility" and "The Great Positive Possibility" in K. Barth, *The Epistle to the Romans,* trans. E. C. Hoskyn (London: Oxford University Press, 1960), 475-502 (hereafter cited as *Romans*).

2. P. Lehmann, "Karl Barth, Theologian of Permanent Revolution," *Union Seminary Quarterly Review* 28 (1972); F.-W. Marquardt, "Socialism in the Theology of Karl Barth," in *Karl Barth and Radical Politics,* ed. G. Hunsinger (Philadelphia: Westminster Press, 1976), 47-76.

3. F.-W. Marquardt, *Theologie und Sozialismus: Das Beispiel Karl Barths* (Munich: Chr. Kaiser Verlag, 1972), 16. Abstracted as "Sozialismus bei Karl Barth," in *Junge Kirche,* 33 (1972), and translated as in note 2.

4. E. Troeltsch, *Der Historismus und Seine Probleme* (Aalen: Scientia Verlag, 1961), 6. Quoted from the translation by P. Lehmann in "Karl Barth, Theologian," 71.

5. K. Barth, *Church Dogmatics* II/1 (Edinburgh: T. & T. Clark, 1957), 386 (hereafter cited as *CD*).

6. Barth, *Romans,* v.

7. Barth, *CD* II/1 (1957), 75.

8. K. Barth, *The Word of God and the Word of Man* (New York: Harper & Row, 1957). See also the preface to the second edition of *Romans*, 2-15.

9. K. Barth, *Final Testimonies* (Grand Rapids: Eerdmans, 1977), 24.

10. Quoted in J. Deschner, "Karl Barth as Political Activist," *Union Seminary Quarterly Review* 28 (Fall 1972): 55.

11. Marquardt, *Theologie und Sozializmus;* E. Busch, *Karl Barth: His Life from Letters and Autobiographical Texts*, trans. J. Bowden (Philadelphia: Fortress Press, 1976).

12. See a review of E. Thurneysen's *Karl Barth: Theologie und Sozialismus, den Briefen seiner Fruhzeit* in the *Scottish Journal of Theology* 27 (1974).

13. Marquardt in Hunsinger, *Barth and Radical Politics*, 59.

14. Ibid., 66.

15. Barth, "Jesus Christ and the Movement for Social Justice," in Hunsinger, ed., *Barth and Radical Politics*, 19.

16. Ibid., 26. Cf. K. Marx, "Contribution to the Critique of Hegel's Philosophy of the Right," in *Karl Marx and Friedrich Engels on Religion*, ed. R. Niebuhr (New York: Schocken Books, 1964). See also K. Marx, *The First International and After, Political Writings*, vol. 3 (New York: Vintage Books, 1974), 324.

17. Barth in Hunsinger, ed., *Barth and Radical Politics*, 26-36. See also *Word of God and Word of Man*, 18. Italics are added.

18. I will refer to this christological revision in the latter part of this essay.

19. Barth, *Word of God and Word of Man*, 299.

20. Ibid., 57. See also *Theologie und Sozialismus*, 145.

21. Barth, *Romans*, 463.

22. Barth, *Word of God and Word of Man*, 120.

23. Ibid., 299.

24. E. Jüngel, *Gottes Sein ist im Werden* (Tübingen: J. C. B. Mohr, 1965).

25. K. Barth, "Der Christelike Glaube und der Geschichte," *Schweizerische Theologische Zeitschrift* (1912). See Hunsinger, "Toward a Radical Barth," in Hunsinger, ed., *Barth and Radical Politics*, 193.

26. K. Barth, "Der Glaube an den Personlichen Gott," *Zeitschrift für Theologie und Kirche* 24 (1914). Quoted by Hunsinger in *Barth and Radical Politics*, 194-95.

27. Ibid.

28. Hunsinger, "Toward a Radical Barth," in Hunsinger, ed., *Barth and Radical Politics*, 215-16.

29. K. Barth, *Theology and Church* (London: SCM, 1962), 226.

30. Barth, *Romans*, 430.

31. Ibid., 234.

32. P. Lehmann, "The Ant and the Emperor," in *How Karl Barth Changed My Mind*, ed. Donald K. McKim (Grand Rapids: Eerdmans, 1986). For Barth's discussion on analogy see K. Barth, *Anselm: Fides Quarens Intellectum* (New York: World Publishing, 1962).

33. M. Horkheimer, "Die Sehnsucht nach dem ganz Andern: ein Interview mit Kommentaar von Helmut Gumnoir" (Hamburg: Furche, 1975), 60.

34. Barth, *Word of God and Word of Man*, 305.

35. K. Barth, *How I Changed My Mind,* Introduction and Epilogue by John D. Godsey (Edinburgh: St. Andrew Press, 1966), 46.

36. Barth, *CD* II/2 (1957), 289; "The Church and the Political Question of Today" (12 Dec. 1938), in *Eine Schweitzer Stimme* (Zumurich: A. G. Zollikon, 1945).

37. See Karl Barth's letter written to Eberhard Bethge on 22 May 1967 after reading his biography of Dietrich Bonhoeffer. This letter was published as part of the proceedings of the Lutheran Synod of Rheinland-Westphalen, January 1980.

38. Barth, CD II/1 (1957), 444.

39. Barth, *Final Testimonies,* 25. See also Lehmann, "The Ant and the Emperor" and "Karl Barth, Theologian," 79.

40. Barth, *Romans,* 475-502.

41. Lehmann, *Transfiguration of Politics,* xiii.

42. J. Cone, "Theology as the Expression of God's Liberating Activity for the Poor," in *The Vocation of the Theologian,* ed. T. W. Jennings (Philadelphia: Fortress Press, 1985), 122, 125, 127.

43. G. Hunsinger, "Karl Barth and Liberation Theology," *Journal of Religion* 63 (July 1983): 260-61.

44. H. Gollwitzer, "Kingdom of God and Socialism in the Theology of Karl Barth," in Hunsinger, ed., *Barth and Radical Politics,* 106.

45. Barth, *Romans,* 493, 496.

46. K. Barth, *Ethics* (Edinburgh: T. & T. Clark, 1981), 163-73.

47. Barth, *CD* III/4 (1961), 534. See also *Eine Schweitzer Stimme, 1938–45.*

48. Barth, *Ethics,* 173.

49. K. Barth, "Church and State," in *Community, State and Church,* ed. W. Herberg (Garden City, N.Y.: Anchor Books, 1960), 101-2.

50. Barth, *Word of God and Word of Man,* 295.

51. Barth, *CD* II/1 (1957), 386.

52. Ibid., 493.

53. P. Tillich, "What is Wrong with Dialectical Theology," *Journal of Religion* 15 (April 1935): 135.

54. Hunsinger in Hunsinger, ed., *Barth and Radical Politics,* 185; Marquardt, *Theologie und Sozialismus,* 165.

55. K. Barth, "The Freedom of Mozart," in *Religion and Culture: Essays in Honour of Paul Tillich,* ed. W. Leibrecht (New York: Harper and Brothers, 1959), 76-77.

56. G. K. Roberts, *A Dictionary of Political Analysis* (London: Longmans, 1971), A9.

57. Barth, "Church and State," in Herberg, ed., *Community, State and Church,* 139.

58. Barth, *Romans,* 484, 491. Italics are added.

59. Barth, *Ethics,* 168.

60. Barth, *Word of God and Word of Man,* 298-99.

61. Ibid., 298.

62. Barth, "The Christian Community and the Civil Community," in Herberg, ed., *Community, State and Church,* 149-89.

63. Barth, *CD* IV/2 (1958), 721.

64. Barth, *CD* IV/1 (1956), 121.

65. K. Marx, "Theses on Feuerbach," in *Writings of the Young Marx on Philosophy and Society,* ed. L. Easton and K. Guddat (Garden City, N.Y.: Doubleday-Anchor, 1967), 400.

66. R. Petersen, *An Analysis of the Nature and Basis of Karl Barth's Socialism,* MA thesis, University of Cape Town (1985).

67. Marquardt in Hunsinger, ed., *Barth and Radical Politics,* 58.

68. Barth, *CD* I/2 (1956), 161.

69. Barth, *CD* II/2 (1957), 577-78.

70. Barth, *CD* III/2 (1960), 217; I/2, 166.

71. Barth, *CD* IV/1 (1956), 186.

72. Ibid., 219.

73. Barth, *CD* IV/2 (1958), 180.

74. J. Cone, *My Soul Looks Back* (Maryknoll, N.Y.: Orbis Books, 1986), 44.

Notes to
Theology and Socialism

1. J. L. Segundo, "Capitalism-Socialism: A Theological Crux," *Concilium,* vol. 6, part 10 (1974): 105-23.

2. F.-W. Marquardt, *Theologie und Sozialismus: Das Bespiel Karl Barths* (Munich: Chr. Kaiser Verlag, 1972) and G. Hunsinger, ed., *Karl Barth and Radical Politics* (Philadelphia: Westminster Press, 1976).

3. This essay is a summary of my "An Analysis of the Nature and Basis of Karl Barth's Socialism" (MA thesis, UCT, 1985).

4. P. Lehmann, "Karl Barth, Theologian of Permanent Revolution," *Union Seminary Quarterly Review* 28 (1972).

5. In Hunsinger, ed., *Barth and Radical Politics.*

6. Ibid., 192-227.

7. Ibid., 203.

8. K. Barth, *Final Testimonies* (Grand Rapids: Eerdmans, 1977), 39.

9. In Hunsinger, ed., *Barth and Radical Politics,* 332.

10. Ibid., 19-46.

11. Ibid., 29.

12. K. Barth, *The Epistle to the Romans* (London: Oxford University Press, 1933), 498.

13. In Hunsinger, ed., *Barth and Radical Politics,* 68; Marquardt, *Theologie und Sozialismus,* 110-11.

14. Hunsinger, ed., *Barth and Radical Politics,* 67.

15. J. D. Smart, ed., *Revolutionary Theology in the Making* (London: Epworth Press, 1964), 19.

16. See K. Barth, *The Humanity of God* (London: Collins, 1961), 14.

17. K. Barth, *Theology and Church* (London: SCM, 1972), 231.

18. Ibid., 231.

19. Ibid., 234.

20. For a fuller account of this correspondence, see Hunsinger, ed., *Barth and Radical Politics*, 116.

21. In W. Herberg, ed., *Community, State and Church* (Garden City, N.Y.: Anchor Books, 1960), 173.

22. In K. Barth, *Against the Stream* (London: SCM, 1954), 107.

23. See, e.g., C. West, *Communism and the Theologians* (London: SCM, 1958), 313; Herberg, ed., *Community, State and Church*, 57.

24. R. McAfee Brown, ed., *How to Serve God in a Marxist Land* (New York: Association Books, 1959), 36ff.

25. K. Barth, *How I Changed my Mind* (Edinburgh: St. Andrew Press, 1969), 57.

26. In Hunsinger, ed., *Barth and Radical Politics*, 19-37; K. Barth, *The Word of God and the Word of Man* (New York: Harper & Row, 1957), 275ff., and in Herberg, ed., *Community, State and Church*, where it appears as "Church and State."

27. In Hunsinger, ed., *Barth and Radical Politics*, 21.

28. Barth, *Word of God and Word of Man*, 276.

29. In Herberg, ed., *Community, State and Church*. A further quotation from *CD* IV/3 affirms this common intention, when speaking of the possibility of the church hearing a "true word" from the secular world. Here Barth specifically mentions socialism, stating that "the features of all of them [true words] . . . is that they point to something *lasting, permanent and constant*" (p. 142; emphasis mine).

30. "The Christian Community and the Civil Community," in Herberg, ed., *Community, State and Church*, 160.

31. E. Thurneysen, *Karl Barth: Theologie und Sozialismus, den Briefen seiner Bruhzeit*, as reviewed by H. Hartwell in *Scottish Journal of Theology* 27 (1974): 95.

32. H. Ur van Balthasar, *The Theology of Karl Barth* (New York: Linehart & Winston, 1971), 151.

33. K. Barth, *Final Testimonies*, 24.

34. Tambach Lecture, in Hunsinger, ed., *Barth and Radical Politics*, 302, 308.

Notes to
Theology and Violence

1. *Confessing and Resisting: The Barmen Declaration* (Johannesburg: SACC, 1984).

2. K. Barth, *The Christian Life* (Grand Rapids: Eerdmans, 1981), 173ff.

3. See C. Villa-Vicencio's more comprehensive discussion on the revolution of God elsewhere in this volume.

4. K. Barth, *Church Dogmatics* IV/2 (Edinburgh: T. & T. Clark, 1958), 180.

5. Barth, *CD* II/1 (1957), 386.

6. See G. Hunsinger, *Karl Barth and Radical Politics* (Philadelphia: West-minster Press, 1976), 225.

7. K. Barth, *The Epistle to the Romans* (London: Oxford University Press, 1933), 480.

8. Barth, *Christian Life,* 174.

9. Barth, *CD* II/1, 386.

10. K. Barth, *Ethics* (Edinburgh: T. & T. Clark, 1981), 446.

11. W. Herberg, ed., *Community, Church and State* (Garden City, N.Y.: Anchor Books, 1960).

12. See P. Lehmann, *The Transfiguration of Politics* (New York: Harper & Row, 1975), 39.

13. K. Barth, *The Knowledge of God and the Service of God According to the Teaching of the Reformation* (London: Hodder & Stoughton, 1938), 229.

14. Ibid., 231.

15. In the analysis of the *Grenzfall* I am indebted to E. Williams for his un-published thesis "A Critical Appraisal of the *Grenzfall* in Karl Barth's Ethics," UNISA, 1981.

16. Barth, *CD* III/4 (1961), 336.

17. Ibid., 342.

18. Ibid., 343.

19. John Howard Yoder in his book *Karl Barth and the Problem of War* (Nashville: Abingdon Press, 1970) argues that there is a basic inconsistency in Barth's approach. He suggests that Barth sets out to proclaim the freedom of God but at times reflects no more than "the autonomy of pragmatic political judge-ment" (p. 115). Yoder argues that it would be more "Barthian" to posit a norma-tive position of Christian pacifism on the basis of the Word of God in which no *Grenzfall* is entertained. My contention here is that Barth believes that the com-mand of God is heard in a specific context. The human context and the divine command cannot be separated. God's absolute freedom can in a sense be appre-ciated only in relation to finite human freedom. There will therefore inevitably be a dialectic between the absolute command of God and the human perception of that command. It is not unnatural to assume that this human perception will at times reflect "practical political judgements." This does not alter the basic pas-sion of Barth's approach, namely, only God is absolute. Only the command of God is normative. No human formulation of the command of God can be given absolute status. God is free to command differently from the way in which the command has generally been perceived. We may wish to disagree with Barth's formulation of God's command, but we must maintain the theological imperative of the freedom of God.

20. D. B. Stoesz, "Karl Barth's Theological Justification of World War II," *ARC,* vol. 12, no. 1 (Autumn 1985): 21-32.

21. Barth, *CD* III/4, 453.

22. Ibid., 455.

23. Ibid., 459.

24. Ibid., 465.

25. Ibid., 466.

26. Barth, *Knowledge,* 229.

27. Ibid., 231.

28. Ibid., 232.

29. Herberg, ed., *Community, Church and State,* 179.

30. J. Moltmann, *On Human Dignity* (London: SCM, 1984), 95.

31. Stoesz, "Karl Barth's Theological Justification," 29.

32. Yoder, *Karl Barth and the Problem of War,* 41.

33. Ibid., 30.

34. D. Bonhoeffer, *Ethics* (New York: Macmillan, 1955), 248.

35. See an excellent preliminary discussion of the issues involved in choosing a sociological model for analysis in J. Míguez-Bonino, *Toward a Christian Political Ethic* (Philadelphia: Fortress Press, 1983), 44-47.

Notes to
Romans 13: A Hermeneutic for Church and State

1. E. Busch, *Karl Barth: His Life from Letters and Autobiographical Texts,* trans. J. Bowden (Philadelphia: Fortress Press, 1976), 81.

2. The first edition of this work has never been translated into English, and therefore I have used K. Barth, *Der Römerbrief* (Erste Fassung), Karl Barth-Gesamtausgabe (Zürich: Theologischer Verlag, 1985) when referring to the first edition. The page numbers in brackets refer to the original printing of the work. For the second edition I have used K. Barth, *The Epistle to the Romans,* trans. E. C. Hoskyn (London: Oxford University Press, 1933).

3. This lecture can be found in K. Barth, *The Word of God and the Word of Man,* trans. D. Horton (New York: Harper & Row, 1957), 28-50.

4. Ibid., 43.

5. Ibid., esp. 45.

6. Ibid., 34-37.

7. Ibid., 34.

8. Barth, *Romans,* 1.

9. Ibid.

10. See F.-W. Marquardt, *Theologie und Sozialismus: Das Beispiel Karl Barths,* 3d ed. (Munich: Chr. Kaiser Verlag, 1985), 124-41.

11. Barth, *Romans,* 501 [376].

12. Ibid., 503 [377].

13. Ibid., 505 [378-79].

14. Ibid., 506 [379].

15. Ibid., 520-21 [390].

16. Ibid., 506-7 [379].

17. G. Hunsinger, "Towards a Radical Barth," in *Karl Barth and Radical Politics,* ed. G. Hunsinger (Philadelphia: Westminster Press, 1976), 208-9. Hunsinger (p. 210), following Marquardt, *Theologie und Sozialismus,* asserts that although Barth felt a conceptual dissatisfaction with his earlier work, the real impetus for rewriting *Romans* was his political disillusionment with, among other things, the Russian revolution, which had degenerated into a police state.

18. See Hunsinger, "Towards a Radical Barth," 204-11.

19. H. U. von Balthasar, *The Theology of Karl Barth,* trans. J. Drury (New

York: Holt, Rinehart, and Winston, 1971), 63. For an important critical discussion of Barth's dialectic method see pp. 53-73.

20. Barth, *Romans,* 461.

21. Ibid., 476-77.

22. Ibid., 478-79.

23. Ibid., 480-81.

24. Ibid., 481.

25. J. D. Smart, *The Interpretation of Scripture* (London: SCM, 1962), 43.

26. This essay is most easily accessible in English under the title "Church and State" in *Community, State, and Church: Three Essays,* ed. W. Herberg (Garden City, N.Y.: Anchor Books, 1960), 101-48.

27. W. Herberg, "The Social Philosophy of Karl Barth," in ibid., 24-29, provides a good introduction to both the Roman Catholic Church's understanding of church and state and the Reformers' views. Herberg notes that Barth rejected the former because it was based in natural theology, and the latter because it distinguished too sharply between creation and redemption, thereby failing to be sufficiently christocentric.

28. Busch, *Karl Barth,* 288.

29. D. F. Ford, "Barth's Interpretation of the Bible," in *Karl Barth: Studies of his Theological Method,* ed. S. W. Sykes (Oxford: Clarendon Press, 1979), 58.

30. See the telling criticism of Barth's use of the Jesus-Pilate episode in J. Bowden, *Karl Barth: Theologian* (London: SCM, 1983), 71.

31. R. E. Hood, "Karl Barth's Christological Basis for the State and Political Praxis," *Scottish Journal of Theology* 33 (1980): 223-38.

32. Barth, "Church and State," 114-16.

33. Ibid., 118.

34. Ibid., 120.

35. Ibid., 128-30.

36. Ibid., 138.

37. Ibid., 139-40.

38. Ibid., 141.

39. Ibid., 147-48.

40. Ibid., 144.

41. Ibid., 145.

42. K. Barth, *Church Dogmatics,* II/1 (Edinburgh: T. & T. Clark, 1957), 386.

43. See P. Lapide, "No Balm in Barmen? A Jewish Debit Account," *Journal of Theology for Southern Africa* 50 (March 1985): 37-51.

44. C. Villa-Vicencio, "Theology in the Service of the State: The Steyn and Eloff Commissions," in C. Villa-Vicencio and J. W. de Gruchy, eds., *Resistance and Hope* (Cape Town: David Philip; Grand Rapids: Eerdmans, 1985), 112-25.

45. Barth's rejection of the state's right to control the church and the church's abdication to that power in Nazi Germany is what led Barth to play an instrumental role in the formation of the Confessing Church.

46. In September 1938 Barth applied his study "Church and State" to the situation in Czechoslovakia by writing that the Czech soldiers would be fighting

not only for freedom but for the Christian church in resisting Hitler. See Busch, *Karl Barth*, 289.

47. See J. Barr, *Old and New in Interpretation: A Study of the Two Testaments*, 2d ed. (London: SCM, 1982), 90-96 and Ford, "Barth's Interpretation," 82-87 for valuable critiques of Barth's interpretation of the Bible.

Notes to
From Barmen to Belhar and Kairos

1. A. Cochrane, *The Church's Confessions Under Hitler* (Philadelphia: Westminster Press, 1962), 92.

2. E. Bethge, *Bonhoeffer: Exile and Martyr* (London: Collins, 1975).

3. K. Barth, *Theologische Existenz Heute* 1933 (1) in K. Barth and E. Thurneyson, *Theologische Existenz Heute* (Munich: Chr. Kaiser Verlag, 1980), 12.

4. D. Bax, *A Different Gospel* (Johannesburg: The Presbyterian Church of Southern Africa, n.d.).

5. W. P. Esterhuyzen, *Afskeid van Apartheid* (Cape Town: Tafelberg, 1979).

6. Cochrane, *Church's Confessions*, 75ff.

7. H. Asmussen, quoted in Cochrane, ibid., 253.

8. Cochrane, *Church's Confessions*, 255.

9. J. de Gruchy, "Towards a Confessing Church," in J. de Gruchy and C. Villa-Vicencio, eds., *Apartheid is a Heresy* (Grand Rapids: Eerdmans; Cape Town: David Philip, 1983), 77.

10. R. W. Lovin, "The Christian and the Authority of the State: Bonhoeffer's Reluctant Revision," *Journal of Theology for Southern Africa* (March 1981), 39.

11. G. Leibholz, in D. Bonhoeffer, *The Cost of Discipleship* (London: SCM Press, 1964), 24f.

12. K. Barth, *Church Dogmatics* II: "The Doctrine of God" (Edinburgh: T. & T. Clarke, 1957), 173.

13. Ibid., 173.

14. Cochrane, *Church's Confessions*, 287.

15. J. Hamel, *"Wärhnemung gesellschaftlicher Verantwordung durch die Evangelische Kirchen in Deutschland—ein Ruckblick,"* in *Aum politischen Auftrag der Christlichen Gemeide Barmen II,* ed. A. Burgmüller (Gütersloh: Gütersloher Verlagshaus Gerd Mohn, 1974), 15.

16. W. Krech, "Das Verständnis von Barmen II unter dem Stickwort 'Königsherrschaft Jesu Christi,'" in ibid., 66.

17. K. Barth, *Church and State* (Gloucester: Peter Smith, 1968), 122-35.

18. H. Asmussen, in Cochrane, *Church's Confessions*, 256.

19. E. Busch, *Karl Barth's Lebenslauf* (Munich: Chr. Kaiser Verlag, 1975), 266.

20. Cochrane, *Church's Confessions*, 258.

21. Barth, *Theologische Existenz Heute*, 14.

22. H. Gollwitzer, *Zuspruch und Anspruch* (Munich: Chr. Kaiser Verlag, 1968), 233.

23. U. Dannemann, *Theologie und Politik in Denken Karl Barths* (Munich: Chr. Kaiser Verlag, 1977), 125.

24. M. Brinkman, *Karl Barths socialistiese Stellingname* (Baarn: Ten Have, 1982), 90.

25. Cochrane, *Church's Confessions,* 261.

26. Ibid., 285.

27. Ibid., 283.

28. See de Gruchy's discussion of B. Naudé, "Die Tyd vir 'n Belydende Kerk is Daar," in de Gruchy and Villa-Vicencio, eds., *Apartheid is a Heresy* (Cape Town: David Philip; Grand Rapids: Eerdmans, 1983), 75ff.

29. N.G. Sendingkerk, "Skema van werksaamhede en handelinge van die drie-en-twintigste hoogeerwaarde sinode van die Nederduitse Gereformeerde Sendingkerk in SA" (Sept.-Oct. 1982).

30. G. D. Cloete and D. J. Smit, eds., *'n Oomblik van Waarheid* (Cape Town: Tafelberg, 1984). *A Moment of Truth* (Grand Rapids: Eerdmans, 1984).

31. Ibid., 164.

32. Ibid., 35.

33. J. de Gruchy, *Bonhoeffer and South Africa: Theology and Dialogue* (Grand Rapids: Eerdmans, 1984), 135-37.

34. A. H. Lückhoff, *Cottesloe* (Cape Town: Tafelburg, 1978).

35. D. F. M. Strauss, *Versoening en Samelewing,* unpublished, Jan. 1984, 10.

36. D. J. Smit, "What Does *Status Confessionis* Mean?" and "'In a Special Way the God of the Destitute, the Poor, and the Wronged,'" in Cloete and Smit, *A Moment of Truth,* 7 and 53.

37. De Gruchy, *Bonhoeffer and South Africa,* 137.

38. K. Barth, "Jesus Christ and the Movement for Social Justice," in *Karl Barth and Radical Politics,* ed. G.Hunsinger (Philadelphia: Westminster, 1976), 19.

39. Ibid., 19-20.

40. Ibid., 22.

41. Ibid., 21.

42. Ibid., 37.

43. H. Gollwitzer, *An Introduction to Protestant Theology* (Philadelphia: Westminster, 1982), 195f.

Notes to
Church and State in South Africa

1. J. de Gruchy and C. Villa-Vicencio, eds., *Apartheid is a Heresy* (Cape Town: David Philip; Grand Rapids: Eerdmans, 1983). See also T. D. Moodie, *The Rise of Afrikanerdom* (Berkeley: University of California Press, 1950), 52-72.

2. J. J. F. Durand, "Afrikaner Piety and Dissent," in *Resistance and Hope,* ed. C. Villa-Vicencio and J. de Gruchy (Grand Rapids: Eerdmans, 1985), 40.

3. W. Abbott, *Documents of Vatican II* (London: Chapman, 1967), 199-308. See also A. Dulles, *A Church to Believe In* (New York: Crossroad, 1983).

4. See discussion of Luther's two-kingdom doctrine in J. Moltmann, *On Human Dignity: Political Theology and Ethics* (London: SCM, 1981). Also U. Duchrow, *Zwei Reiche und Regimente* (Gütersloh: Gütersloher Verlagshaus Gerd Mohn, 1977).

5. J. Calvin, *Institutes of the Christian Religion,* ed. J. T. McNeill, vol. 2 (Philadelphia: Westminster Press, 1973), Book 4, Chapter XX, pp. 1485ff.

6. For A. Van Ruler's model see *Gestaltwerdung Christi in der Welt* (Nijkerk: Callenbach, 1956).

7. A useful introduction to Kuyper's church-state doctrine is found in A. Kuyper, *Lectures on Calvinism* (Grand Rapids: Eerdmans, 1970).

8. H. Thielicke, *Theological Ethics,* vol. 2, *Politics* (Grand Rapids: Eerdmans, 1969), 598-604.

9. A. Kuyper, *De Gemeene Gratie* (Kampen, n.d.), 646-53.

10. J. J. F. Durand, "The Prophetic Task of the Church vis-à-vis the State," in *Church and Nation,* Theological Conference Papers, Reformed Ecumenical Synod (1981), 8.

11. W. Herberg, ed., *Community, State and Church* (New York: Anchor Books, 1960), 149-89.

12. This is discussed in Moodie, *Rise of Afrikanerdom.*

13. D. J. Bosch, A. König, and W. D. Nichol, eds., *Perspektief op die Ope Brief* (Cape Town: Human & Rousseau, 1982).

14. K. Barth, *Church Dogmatics* II: "The Doctrine of God" (Edinburgh: T. & T. Clark, 1955), 386.

15. This point is further discussed in C. Villa-Vicencio's essay "Karl Barth's Revolution of God: Quietism or Anarchy?", elsewhere in this volume.

16. A. Kuyper, *Christianity and the Class Struggle* (Grand Rapids: Eerdmans, 1950).

Notes to
Racism, Reconciliation, and Resistance

1. B. B. Keet, "Honderd jaar van teologie in voëlvlug," *Ned. Geref. Teologiese Tydskrif* 2 (March 1960).

2. B. B. Keet, *Whither South Africa?* (Stellenbosch: University Publishers, 1955). See J. J. F. Durand, "Afrikaner Piety and Dissent," in C. Villa-Vicencio and J. W. de Gruchy, eds., *Resistance and Hope: South African Essays in Honour of Beyers Naudé* (Cape Town: David Philip; Grand Rapids: Ecrdmans, 1985), 45-46.

3. E. Jüngel, "Karl Barth zu Ehren," in *Karl Barth: 1886–1968* (Zürich, 1968), 50. Quoted by Paul Lehmann in "Karl Barth, Theologian of Permanent Revolution," *Union Seminary Quarterly Review* 28 (1972): 81.

4. Karl Barth, "The Desirability and Possibility of a Universal Reformed Creed," in *Theology and Church* (London: SCM, 1962), 133.

5. See my essay, "Towards a Confessing Church: the Implications of a Heresy," in J. W. de Gruchy and C. Villa-Vicencio, eds., *Apartheid is a Heresy* (Cape Town: David Philip; Grand Rapids: Eerdmans, 1983).

6. B. J. Marais, *Colour: Unsolved Problem of the West* (Cape Town: Howard Timmins, 1952), 301ff.

7. K. Barth, *CD* IV/1, 703.

8. Barth, *CD* III/4, 479.

9. I am indebted at this point to Professor Clifford Green's response to my presentation of this paper at the Barth Symposium, Stony Point, New York, May 1986.

10. See esp. Barth, *CD* III/2, 45.

11. K. Barth, *Ethics* (Edinburgh: T. & T. Clark, 1981), 164.

12. J. Cone, *Black Theology and Black Power* (New York: Seabury Press, 1969), 143ff.

13. "The Kairos Document, Article 3.1," *Journal of Theology for Southern Africa* 53 (Dec. 1985).

14. J. Moltmann, "Barth's Doctrine of the Lordship of Jesus Christ," in J. Moltmann, *On Human Dignity: Political Theology and Ethics* (Philadelphia: Fortress Press, 1984), 89.

15. Barth, *CD* IV/2, 620.

16. See J. Lochman, *Reconciliation and Liberation* (Philadelphia, 1980), which is written from the perspective of Barth's theology.

17. See, e.g., K. Barth, "The Christian Community and the Civil Community," in *Against the Stream* (London: SCM, 1954), 19, 22-23.

18. Barth, *CD* II/1, 386-87.

19. Contained in an Appendix in Barth, *A Letter to Great Britain from Switzerland* (London: Sheldon Press, 1941), 34.

20. K. Barth, "Church and State," in *Community, State and Church*, ed. W. Herberg (Garden City, N.Y.: Anchor Books, 1960), 106.

21. Barth, in Herberg, ed., *Community, State and Church*, 114.

22. Barth, "Christian Comunity and Civil Community," 24.

23. See Moltmann, *On Human Dignity*, 85.

24. Barth, in Herberg, ed., *Community, State and Church*, 119-20.

25. Barth, *Against the Stream*, 34.

26. Barth, in Herberg, ed., *Community, State and Church*, 123.

27. Ibid., 146.

28. Ibid., 143.

29. Barth, *Ethics*, 158.

30. Barth, *Against the Stream*, 35-36.

31. See Barth, *CD* IV/4, 205ff.

32. See Barth, *Against the Stream*, 17.

33. Barth, in Herberg, ed., *Community, State and Church*, 139.

34. See A. Boesak and C. Villa-Vicencio, *When Prayer Makes News* (Philadelphia: Westminster Press, 1986).

35. Barth, *Letter to Great Britain from Switzerland*, 51.

36. Barth, in Herberg, ed., *Community, State and Church*, 145.

Contributors

Allan Boesak is president of the World Alliance of Reformed Churches and moderator of the N.G. Sendingkerk.

Alan Brews is minister of the Buitenkant Street Methodist Church, Cape Town.

Jaap Durand is deputy vice-chancellor of the University of the Western Cape.

John de Gruchy is professor of Christian Studies, Department of Religious Studies, University of Cape Town.

Nico Horn is pastor of the Apostolic Faith Mission, Krugersdorp, and part-time lecturer in the Department of Systematic Theology at Unisa.

Robin Petersen is minister of the United Congregational Church of Southern Africa, serving the Heideveld United Church.

Dirkie Smit is professor of systematic theology, Theology Faculty, University of the Western Cape.

Charles Villa-Vicencio is associate professor, Department of Religious Studies, University of Cape Town.

C. A. Wanamaker is senior lecturer, Department of Religious Studies, University of Cape Town.